Mental Retardation: Present and Future Perspectives

Henry Leland
The Ohio State University

Daniel E. Smith
Parsons State Hospital and Training Center, Kansas

Charles A. Jones Publishing Company
Worthington, Ohio

This book is dedicated to all mentally retarded and developmentally disabled persons whose lives the authors have unwittingly jeopardized through institutionalization.

1 2 3 4 5 6 7 8 9 10 / 78 77 76 75 74

Library of Congress Catalog Card Number: 74-77631
International Standard Book Number: 0-8396-0048-8

Printed in the United States of America

Preface

Mental Retardation: Present and Future Perspectives is a book for those who want to understand and improve the care and rehabilitation of the mentally retarded. As a resource, it is indispensable for those training in the helping professions in colleges and universities, at the graduate and undergraduate levels. Those students in associate degree programs and in junior and technical colleges should find it especially helpful as a basic text. It also will be useful to those who have some contact with the problems of retardation and wish to extend their background on the subject—such as social workers, teachers, counselors, physicians, and nurses, including public health nurses and pediatric nurse associates.

Further, this book can aid the general reader in understanding what should be done in the community. It will serve parents and parents' groups. It will help school board members, school supervisors, and others who need to reach decisions about programs for the retarded on community and state levels. To better their lives, the retarded need—must have—the aid of all of these people.

Until the 1960's, care and treatment of the retarded was almost entirely centered on institutions, which too often proved debilitating to their residents. New conceptualizations and research have combined to produce the single most significant event of the past decade in the field of mental retardation—the opening of the door to the community. This new orientation has as its basis the vital tenet that the retarded are *people* who belong in the mainstream of community life.

The major purpose of this book is to facilitate the shift to the community of the mentally retarded and the mentally disabled. Therefore we devote the first half of the text to a broad panoramic view of the total situation as it now exists. Along the way we introduce significant professional and social concepts concerning both the retarded and the mentally disabled.

In the second part of the book we describe and discuss many types of programs, services, and facilities that can be provided for the mentally retarded. It is our view that with immediate implementation of these, community living will become possible for thousands who otherwise may spend many long years—even entire lifetimes—in an institution unnecessarily.

As will become even more obvious, the major theme running through the book is that of advocacy for the human rights of the mentally retarded. But more than simply explaining this as a principle, although we do that, it is our purpose to demonstrate how at the community level mechanisms can be devised that make human rights a living reality.

A glossary is provided at the end of the book not only for use in reading the material—in fact we hope that the text is clear enough that the glossary will not be needed often by the reader—but also for reference in other reading. The person who receives periodicals or occasional written material on mental retardation will find this section especially useful, as will also the one who wants to delve further into the references listed.

H. Leland
D. E. Smith
C. A. Crawford

Acknowledgments

For twelve years the authors worked together at Parsons State Hospital and Training Center, Kansas. Parsons is dedicated to research of the problems of mentally retarded, emotionally disturbed, and developmentally disabled youth. Its programs of demonstration and investigation have produced much of the information on which this book is based.

To acknowledge each person who helped prepare this book would require another volume twice the size. We express heartfelt thanks to all of them. Specifically we do acknowledge the tremendous debt we owe the American Association on Mental Deficiency and its membership; the Council for Exceptional Children and its membership; and those members of the American Psychological Association who have supported work in the area of mental retardation and developmental disability, particularly the Child Clinical section of Division Twelve. Special thanks go to the parents of retarded children with whom we have worked over many years; they have had many excellent ideas about what should be happening with their children and have shown great patience with the many imperfections in the professional programs that we and others have imposed upon them.

More specifically, we thank Dr. Howard V. Bair of Parsons State Hospital and Training Center for making the necessary facilities and time available for us to carry on the research and investigation and Dr. William Gibson of The Ohio State University, The Nisonger Center, for making time and equipment available for the completion of this book. Such a book is never written just by the authors; there is always a backup crew. Those who have provided professional input for us have included Antoinette Cyrulik-Jacobs, M.A.; Barbara Edmonson, Ed.D.; Kazuo Nihira, Ph.D.; Sidney L. DeBriere, M.D.; and certainly not least, Helen Leland, M.A., who not only contributed the second chapter but who also with tremendous fortitude worked with us to help avoid the language barbarisms that would otherwise have been present. Very special thanks go to Cecilia Crawford, M.A., our editorial assistant, who besides providing the graphic concepts kept all of the messy details in order. We also recognize the dedication of our secretaries, Bonnie Oden, Doris Kurtz, Frances Thomas, Patricia Bryson, and Berniece Knight. Finally warm thanks go to our reviewers whose valuable advice helped clear many rough edges and complete missing sections—Dr. Elias Katz, Dr. Reginald L. Jones, Dr. Robert L. Erdman, Ms. Ann Mirels, Dr. Eleanor Lynch, and Dr. Theodore Wohl.

Contents

List of Figures

Part One

Present Perspectives

Introduction

Mental retardation[1] is one of the most neglected social problems facing children and parents today. While society lags in furnishing services for disturbed adults, it is even further behind in those that it provides for retarded or handicapped children. Although public awareness and understanding of the problem have greatly increased over the past twenty years, much remains to be done; now we must look carefully at what we have accomplished so far and then decide upon both priorities among the remaining tasks and approaches to those tasks.

Advancing Understanding of Mental Retardation

In 1961, John F. Kennedy appointed the President's Panel on Mental Retardation; its report was published in 1962. The report laid a basis for national understanding of what was known in the field and for national guidelines toward change (Kennedy, 1963). It formulated the ideas for legislative programs of hospital improvement, professional training, and research. Programs for the retarded then became popular; federal and state governments provided money for work in the field; services that had not previously considered mental retardation a part of their mission became interested in it. Major research, **training, rehabilitation,** and

[1]The terms included in the Glossary are printed in **boldface** type the first time they appear.

treatment centers evolved and there was a sudden blossoming of community **day-care centers,** mental retardation (MR) treatment centers, and vocational training centers. **Special educational** facilities expanded throughout all of the states.

At the same time mental retardation began to develop as a discipline whose adherents are professional specialists in the field. Courses of study in mental retardation were added to university curricula, and advanced study, leading to graduate degrees in the subject, became possible.[2]

But having reached this point, do we want to continue in this direction? Certainly we need a continuing expansion of services for the mentally retarded, but is our present approach the best way to deal with the problems? We are trying to apply the modern results of intensive research to an antique **institutional** system, out-of-date attitudes regarding **intelligence** and **behavior,** and old-fashioned practices in child-rearing. These three areas provide some of the most important challenges that we face today. It would appear that new approaches to them may be in order.

As a result of the research and demonstration projects of past years, we have accumulated a large body of knowledge. Now we must begin to use this knowledge to solve problems. This is not to say that basic research must always have an applied reason, but it is to say that when data are available they should be used. In fact, if they are not, the agencies that support the research will in time begin to question its value.

What now must be done is to advance from basic research to applied research that will try out the basic hypotheses in a systematic way, in order to determine which of them are useful and which must be developed further. Then as principles are derived and proven, they must be built into programs of community services which can then begin to solve problems. This movement from basic research to community program development to problem-solving will have to be speeded up, coordinated, and expanded if the MR discipline is to meet its responsibilities to the nation.

[2]Portions of this discussion were presented by Henry Leland as an **American Association on Mental Deficiency,** Region V, Presidential Address (1968).

Further, these actions will demonstrate that the money was well spent and that the nation has benefited in clear-cut, observable ways. One result will be that pleas for increased funds will find a wider and more receptive audience.

Who Should Be Labeled "Retarded"?

When we speak of research and demonstration programs for the retarded, of whom are we talking? Just who are these individuals? They must be identified before we can begin. The American Association on Mental Deficiency (Heber, 1961) established an adequate definition of mental retardation, and in 1973 revised it to read, "significantly subaverage general intellectual functioning existing concurrently with deficits in **adaptive behavior,** and manifested during the developmental period" (Grossman, 1973). It gives a base to anyone who wishes to work with the problem. There remains, however, the question as to just who fits this definition, or to put it more constructively, who would benefit by being so described.

A number of individuals with various handicaps might fit the definition as given. Subaverage general intellectual functioning is usually taken to mean a low **intelligence quotient (IQ).** Using the AAMD 1961 classification, a low IQ may mean anything below 84 on a **Wechsler Test,** or below 83 on the **Binet** and in terms of the current functioning of some school systems it may mean anything into the range of the 90's. Often children with even higher IQ's present clear-cut learning difficulties—difficulties which not only occur during the developmental period but which also frequently seem to begin quite early in that period. These learning difficulties may or may not include an impairment in adaptive behavior, but if they do they could well be the basis, in terms of the AAMD definition, for a **diagnosis** of retardation. Yet such children may be, to quote Jane Mercer, "mentally retarded only six hours a day,"[3] or in other words when they are in school.

If a child has such difficulties only in school and if outside it he meets the demands of situations effectively, he probably

[3]Personal communication, April, 1968, University of California at Riverside.

should not be labeled as mentally retarded. The label may become the basis for denying services that are not in any way connected to retardation; there still are places where retarded children do not receive the same prosthetic services that normal children receive, and there still are state laws that limit services according to IQ. In addition, there usually are social situations in which such a label causes strong bias against the child and leads to the supposition that his deficiency is irreversible.

Then there are a vast number of people who may meet the definition, but who are relatively invisible within their usual environments. Most of them have already demonstrated that they can function in a normal work or community situation. It would be highly destructive to attempt to make a national registry of mental retardation; it would do a great disservice to both the individuals and the community.

We therefore need to identify those particular people who might benefit from being called retarded. It is not the word that causes the difficulty. Various nations and organizations use a large number of terms such as mentally deficient, feebleminded, and oligophrenic, as well as mentally retarded. The definition is intended to serve as an operational label, and the question should not be "what is the label?" but rather "who receives it?" Generally speaking it should be those who, because of their retardation, are "visible."

The concept of **visibility** is related both to creativity and to survival. If behavior is distributed on some sort of curve, no matter how skewed it may be, most people are found to behave within a normal mode and act as relatively invisible parts of society. Others, extremely creative individuals, perform on an above-normal basis, and visibility is their stock in trade; to survive they must be visible and must sell their creativity—or at least the idea that they are creative. At the other end of the curve are those who function on a subnormal basis. To them visibility is destructive; as long as they remain invisible they are treated as though they are fairly normal, but when their behavior attracts attention they are put away in institutions or at least out of the public eye (Leland & Smith, 1965, pp. 31-33; Shellhaas & Nihira, 1969).

But many children who are not retarded may still function subnormally and become visible for a number of reasons; the problem is to give them a useful operational label. For example, a child who is primarily in need of seizure control if his difficulty is not carefully analyzed, may be classified as retarded and given services that he does not need and that do not help him. Similarly, a child whose visibility is based on emotional disruption and who cannot read because of an emotional learning block certainly ought not to be grouped with the retarded.

Identifying the Retarded

The major difference between the mentally retarded child and any other child is that the former, when left to his own devices, is unable to utilize the cues and stimuli from his surroundings as appropriate guides to behavior (Leland, 1964). His visibility is based more on his inability to know that **cues** are present or that there are decisions to be made than it is on misusing cues, as does the bright but emotionally disturbed child. For instance, a retarded child may step out into a busy street unaware that traffic is a warning cue to which he should attend. The lack of cue identification as a guide to social and personal behavior is one of the main criteria in identifying the child whose behavior is caused by something labeled "retardation." His inability to enter a situation, draw appropriate **social inferences** from it, and establish a behavior course based on those inferences, is characteristic of the retarded person (see Test of Social Inference [TSI] Edmonson, deJung, Leland, & Leach, 1974; Edmonson, Leland, deJung, & Leach, 1967). Such a child will be highly visible because he will be responding in ways that are different from those of his peers.

As he will respond to cues in a different manner, his **reception** of information, his **perception,** his information storage, and his information available for retrieval will all be different from those of a normal child. And of course, so will his overall pattern of **cognition** (Cook, 1966). Thus, although cognitive abilities are present and can be expanded upon, and although through proper clinical intrusion the child can literally be "forced to think" (Leland & Smith,

1965), yet when he is left to his own devices the processes do not go forward at the same pace and in the same manner as with a normal child.

Because of this condition, the child almost certainly will have communication deficiencies. These will lead to more failures in identification and utilization of cues, which in turn will lead to more failures in communication; it is this snowball effect which must be reversed if we are to deal with the problem. The child most apt to benefit from the label of retardation is the one caught in the middle of such a snowball.

Cognitive processes and capacities develop spontaneously with **maturation.** If a child cannot put to use his environmental cues this **development** will not occur or will occur slowly or in a modified way. We must distinguish between what a person actually does and what he is capable of doing. We may say that all children are capable of the highest level of cognitive function, but in actual practice they may not be because of intervening factors. These factors can be of social, intellectual, or physical origin. The concept that at birth a child is relatively immature is an important one. No child is born with all of his faculties intact, as demonstrated by the increase in brain weight and the complexity of brain growth during the first six months of life (Magoun, Darling & Prost, 1960). During this period of physical and intellectual immaturity the child's cognitive processes develop. If his development is somehow impaired, either through the **chaos of sensory** input or in other ways, maturation will be faulty and the child will have increasing difficulties in social communication; the result will be a negative social visibility that will both frighten and annoy the community in which he resides.

The AAMD definition of mental retardation includes the concept of "deficit in adaptive behavior." This concept implies more than merely bad behavior; it implies that the child is unable to **cope** with the natural and social demands of his environment (Nihira, Foster, & Spencer, 1968). It indicates that his cognitive skills have been modified or neglected and he is not able to adapt. Thus we begin to approach a social definition of mental retardation. When society looks at a person, it does not usually attempt to measure his intelligence accurately and it may not know what happened to him during his developmental period, but it sees clearly what he is doing at that particular time, and if he is failing to adapt, it says, "This child is in trouble." If his failure seems related to intellectual slowness (which gives rise to the British term of feeblemindedness) it will say that he is retarded (Gunzberg, 1968).

This failure goes beyond the question of what the child can do. One dimension of adaptive behavior is **independent functioning,** but this is not really what society judges except in the case of children who are not toilet trained or cannot dress or feed themselves. In the older child the independent functioning is not usually impaired; in fact, if he throws a rock through a window we can consider that his independent functioning is in pretty good order. He has to pick up the rock, grasp it, throw it, and if it is to go through the window throw it with some accuracy. What in fact is impaired here is his **personal responsibility.**

Thus, in thinking of a social definition of mental retardation we must think largely of the way that society views the child as he functions in a variety of adaptive situations. The child of low IQ who enters a grocery store but causes no trouble gets no label from the grocer; if, however, the child knocks down a cereal display or a stack of cans, the grocer becomes aware of his presence, and if this sort of thing occurs often the grocer may ask the mother to leave her child at home the next time she comes shopping.

Such a development can raise a series of problems. The grocer has defined the child as socially unacceptable and has set rules concerning the parent's behavior, at least in relationship to her child in his store. The child has created a general disruption which may bother other customers or actually cause boxes or cans to hit them, and which at least will force the assistant to restack the display. The grocer may go home and tell his wife about the child. The widening ripples, particularly if the child causes a number of such incidents, will lead the community to ask the mother to "do something" about her child.

The community thus identifies the child. Then it asks what is wrong with him; is he mentally retarded, emotionally disturbed, or what? But all of this is after the fact; the first step is the identification of the child because of his observed behavior. It is from this frame of reference that one has to approach the question of who is retarded and who needs the services for the retarded.

2

The Development of Terms

The problem of identifying people through words is probably as old as language itself.[1] It has been said that if there were only two people in the world, each would evolve some word that meant the other was foolish. Certainly it is true that language is heavily laden with words intended to somehow classify other people's mentalities.

These classifications are not always pejorative—that is, have a lower, less respectful meaning—but even so they tend to carry a mystical or superstitious meaning. Thus the word *genius* derives from the same source as *genie* or the *jinni* of the Middle East; a genius was thought to possess occult powers and his abilities were explained as deriving from a foreign agent.

This idea developed from an earlier notion that there is a "normal" mentality or behavior and that those who differ from it are unnatural. Aristotle had the concept that unnatural behavior was caused by a foreign spirit, a *dimon,* which had taken possession of the person involved. The word came down to us as *demon* and so did the idea. Until comparatively recently many people died hideously in torture chambers or at the stake as society tried to exorcise these demons. Aristotle perhaps conceived this theory as a way of rationalizing the behavior of his prize pupil,

[1]The following material is drawn from Leland, Helen (1968).

Alexander the Great, who, if we can accept Plutarch's version of his life, behaved in his enjoyment of battlefield bloodbaths as a person whom we today would describe as paranoic.

Even this last sentence illustrates the peculiarities of language in this area. The use of rationalize in the negative sense implies that somehow it is wrong "to be able to reason."

For our purposes here we will concentrate on the development of words chosen to designate subnormal intellects.

There is a tendency for all of us to equate a difference of opinion with the notion that our opponent has an inferior intellect, and many words originated in that way. For example, the word *fatuity* refers both to "obstinacy" and "blind stubbornness" on the one hand, and to "foolishness" and "idiocy" on the other. Thus an obstinate or stubborn opponent is in the same word an idiot.

The word *fatuous* has an interesting history. In Latin it means "foolish" and is said to derive from the seeress Fatua; people were supposedly driven to stupefaction by her prophesies and became "without a mind." This also is the derivation of the word describing that peculiar mindless state of young lovers, *infatuation,* which also gave rise to the Latin pun, *amantes amentis*—"mindless lovers."

At this point another distinction was established, for by describing the fatuous person as mindless he was differentiated from the person who was possessed by demons but who was thought still to retain part of his mind. Thus a *demented* person is considered to have lost part and retained part, though today we usually say that a *dement* has "lost his mind," or going back to a mystical concept, is "out of his mind."

Returning to Fatua, her name also gave us the word *fool* via the peculiarities of the translator's art. In Latin the court jester was called *fatua;* somehow this became confused with "lack of judgment" which actually derived from the Latin *follis*—a bellows or windbag—and the word *fool* was elected to cover both circumstances. The tendency, however, was to emphasize "mindless," and this we find carried on in the

French idea that a mindless person is a *fou* and a mindless group of people, a mob, is a *foule*.

The jester himself acquired another name, *buffoon,* drawing both from the word fool and from *buffa,* to jest. Thus a buffoon becomes one who makes foolish jests. Many of the jesters were in fact noted for their wisdom (reminding us of the Yiddish proverb, "a complete fool is half a prophet") but often were men with misshapen bodies—which reinforced the social stereotype that appearance is related to mentality. Thus we have a French expression, *rire comme un bossu;* literally, "laugh like a hunchback" or actually, laugh in a wild, foolish manner. The composer Verdi made use of this stereotype when he conceived Rigoletto, a laughing, hunchbacked buffoon who, because of Verdi's humanism, was presented as a sympathetic though tragic figure.

When we move from the general concept of foolishness to phrases actually descriptive of the mentally inferior, we encounter a war of words. Present writers describe these people as a group by terms such as *oligophrenic,* which derives from the Greek and means "little mind," and *feebleminded,* which derives from the Latin word *flebelis,* meaning tearful. This word has a similar root to foible, thus implying that a "weakness of character" is similar to tearfulness, and, in present usage, *feeblemindedness.* Here there is an implication that the condition is somehow the person's own fault.

Another common term is *mental deficiency.* The English word deficiency comes from the Latin *deficere,* meaning "to fail." The connotation seems to be that something is lacking, and that it is the ingredient that would lead to success. The term mental deficiency implies that there is a lack of brain, a concept now considered scientifically inaccurate, and so a more common term today is *mental retardation,* which means a "state of being slow." Thus we have moved from a "little mind," through a "weak mind," through a "missing brain," to a "slow mind"—all referring to essentially the same condition.

Terms used to specify various categories within the mentally inferior group are of equally mixed origin. The word *idiot,* for example, comes originally from the Greek *idiote* meaning "private person" or "one's own person"—one separated from other people. The implication of retardation here is completely arbitrary but is of long standing; it is thought that the line of development went from "one's own person," to "common man" in the democratic sense, to "uneducated," to "ignorant" or "ill-informed," and thence to "mental defective." Somewhere along the way there also evolved the word *idiosyncracy* with its idea of peculiar behavior but without any implication of retardation.

The word *imbecile* has a more logical root, the Latin *imbecillus* meaning "weak," but was originally used for any form of debility. It is unclear how it became specifically used for weakness of the mind, but it was generally used to separate individuals whose minds were out of contact with the rest of the world, the idiots, and those who were in contact but were of weak mind, the *imbeciles.*

Moron is a word of disputed origin. One theory derives it from the Greek word *moros,* meaning "dull." But there also is the story that it was coined by Doctor Goddard at Vineland Training School in New Jersey when he translated the Simon-Binet test into English. According to this version, there were three descriptions of mental defectives in use at that time, "idiot," "imbecile," and "moral idiot." (The latter term apparently was coined by Dr. Benjamin Rush, one of the signers of the Declaration of Independence, who is known as the father of American psychiatry.) Goddard is thought to have made a contraction of the last two words for the sake of simplicity and thus to have produced the word *moron.* In any event, Goddard was the first to use the term and thereafter "moral idiocy" disappeared from the literature.

The common school term *dunce* was derived from the name of the philosopher John Duns Scotus who preached during the thirteenth century. He was a scholastic theologian who had very rigid notions; his followers, called Dunsians or Dunses, were associated with the blocking of progressive moves in theology and education. They were described as "stupid enemies of learning" and later as "dull, obstinate persons impervious to learning." It is this last meaning that has been carried forward to the present time and implies a stupid person or *blockhead*—a person whose head is as hard as a block.

As we have seen, many of the common terms associated with mental retardation derive from the appearance of the afflicted person. Perhaps the most common is the term *mongol* or *mongolian* idiot which describes a kind of retarded individual who, though of non-Asiatic origin, seems to have a Chinese or Mongolian appearance of the eyes. Another common term, *gargoyle,* designates a victim of a severely disfiguring disease associated with mental defect, the implication being that such a person somehow resembles the water spouts of Notre Dame de Paris. One of the most interesting words used to describe a condition is *cretin,* which derives from a variation of the French *chretian* or "Christian," and which was used to point out that the dwarfed, misshapen, and extremely ugly victims were really human beings, not animals.

Two other words also seem to owe their usage to the appearance and behavior of those they describe. The first is the word *stupid,* which derives from the Latin *stupidus*—"struck dumb" or "stunned." A speechless, dazed, vacant-looking individual could well be described as being in a stunned condition and thus stupid. Originally it had the connotation of being a temporary condition; and although it still is used in that sense by parents describing their children, through usage it also has acquired the idea of permanence.

A second such word is *dumb,* which means primarily "without speech" or "mute." It is evidently an Old English word similar to the Greek *idiote*. The idea was that speech is a normal characteristic and that one who did not have it was unusual or *dumb*. The German word *dumm,* meaning "stupid" or "foolish," has become mixed up with the English one so that common American usage gives both meanings to the word, with the added connotation that a mute person also is stupid. In a sense both meanings are proper, but not necessarily referring to the same person; one may be deaf and dumb without in any way being a *dumbbell.*

It may be that our failure to choose positive words to describe the mentally retarded has been one of the factors slowing down public interest in the development of appropriate treatment and training programs. The problem of definition and description must be one of continuing concern.

3

Intelligence, Poverty, and Mental Retardation

Intellectual growth within a child is directly affected by many social and environmental factors, among them economic level and **cultural** surroundings. These factors have clear relationships with disease, nutritional deficiencies, and such social ills as alcoholism and drug addiction, all of which contribute to the biological and psychological causes of intellectual degradation (Kugel & Parsons, 1967).

Retardation does in fact occur at all social levels. When we study the lives of Nero and Peter III, we must assume that the retarded have even worn the royal purple; but most elements associated with retardation are accentuated by poverty (Jedrysek, Rosenblatt, & Wortis, 1968). The problem seems to center around a "learning turn-off," caused by socioeconomic factors, a condition that directly affects **academic achievement** even though it occurs long before the child enters school.

What is the actual relationship between intelligence and mental retardation (Leland, 1969a)? Every organism is both **biomedical** and social; one aspect cannot go wrong without influencing the other. Therefore intelligence must include cognition and adaptive behavior, plus **sensory-motor development.** A child cannot develop appropriately in any intellectual sphere if the sensory-motor aspects of his development are impaired.

For example, paralytic polio in an adult person becomes a handicap, but as in the case of Franklin Delano Roosevelt it need not impede any of the higher areas of functioning. However, the same degree of affliction in an infant would seriously impede his ability to develop through **handed experiences** (Weltfish, 1962), and would impair the growth of cognitive processes and could well produce retardation. It is entirely possible that children who are blind, deaf, or have **cerebral palsy** are given the label of retardation because of their sensory-motor impairment, and that without it, the remaining aspects of their functioning might fall within the normal range. Other individuals may have secondary deficiencies such as speech impediments that interfere with communication development (Schiefelbusch, Bair & Spradlin, 1963), coordination difficulties that hinder writing skills, or maldevelopment of internal organs or **epilepsy** that may interfere with the long-range evolution of independent functioning (Pond, 1962). These burdens, placed upon young people who might otherwise be considered below-average but normal, can bring them to a condition of retardation.

Is the IQ Useful?

Measured intelligence, the concept of IQ, is not distributed in a "normal" pattern (Goslin, 1968), and is not a useful diagnostic tool. Intellectual functioning is primarily the ability to cope with the interaction of social and personal forces; intelligent behavior can be defined as successful coping (Leland, 1969a). Using measured intelligence to define retardation is saying that the rate of previous learning—the basis of the IQ—derived from a person's coping and cognitive skills defines those skills. This is somewhat like saying that a house is blue because blue paint was used on it, and that the paint was blue because the resulting house is blue. Yet if blue paint was used, one presumes that the painter had certain underlying reasons for his choice; and if a certain IQ is measured one must presume that there are certain bases for it and that intelligence is to be described not in terms of the IQ, but rather in terms of the learning patterns from which it is derived. If there is a question as to whether or not a child can benefit from certain levels of education in one of the leading universities, an IQ may be useful; but if the question is whether the child can be trained to cross the street by himself or put on his own trousers, the determination of an IQ is pointless.

When IQ's are taken in cases of mental retardation it usually is done because the person measured has been socially visible and is presumed to be retarded, and the person doing the measurement has the justifiable fear that a mistake may have been made. But if we can abandon the notion of automatic separation of an individual from society upon a diagnosis of retardation, then mislabeling is not so serious. And we really do not care whether the grocery display was knocked over by a child with an IQ of 30 or 130; it is the behavior that has to be modified.

Social Intelligence

Another aspect of intelligence is **social intelligence.** A person who is not aware of the mores, laws, and practices of the social environment around him is generally considered less than intelligent, although often people who go to foreign countries show just this same lack of awareness and we do not call them retarded. The problem is to decide how much the lack is related to a total inability to cope with environment. The person in a foreign country usually learns a few words of the language, observes how other people act and follows their examples, and generally adapts to the situation in which he finds himself. The retarded child, however, cannot use environmental cues and draw proper social inferences, and so he cannot evolve a pattern that lets him function socially.

For the retarded a new town, a new section of the old town, or even a new classroom may be like a foreign country; for they present new kinds of social demands. If the retarded person cannot adapt, his behavior may be catastrophic; thus we have parents of retarded children saying that their children act so terrible in public that they must always be kept at home. Or in another case, a child may get just far enough from home that the cues he has been trained to use no longer apply and he becomes lost; his mother, who knows he can readily find his way home within a certain radius, may assume he has run away. She punishes him when she finds him, not realizing that one block beyond his familiar territory the child is in a strange land. The punishment adds the element of injustice to learning deficiency, creating additional blocks and increasing the difficulties of overcoming the real problem.

As society becomes more complex, and as intellectual demands on the individual become more stringent, behavior which at one time was acceptable and average may no longer be so considered. For example, simple jobs requiring muscle power are becoming harder to find. Thus the skills and qualities for which a child's parents were rewarded and given social reinforcement may no longer bring rewards, while at the same time quite different demands are made on the child. Should the parents assume that the skills which brought them recognition and satisfaction will also provide reinforcement to the child, and should they for this reason train him to do the same things, he may find that the expected rewards are not forthcoming and be additionally frustrated.

We see this problem especially in peer **acceptance.** The parents during their childhoods probably had regular chores which were part of family life, and free time was organized around those chores. The less intelligent but stronger child may have been able to finish his chores sooner and thus have more free time than other children, and the others would then envy him and admire his ability. But today such chores are rare and free time is more common; peer acceptance is based less on physical strength and more on a child's abilities to grasp the intricacies of the local games. No matter how much the slow child pleases his parents by doing chores he will not attain peer reinforcement and will be considered "dumb" by his companions.

Mental Retardation and Subcultural Communities

There is an increasing body of data which indicates that children in socially impoverished areas and other concentrations of minorities produce test scores which make them appear to be subaverage (Heber, 1968; Olivier & Barclay, 1967). These data must be considered with those which reveal the extent that malnutrition, "poor **mother power**," disease, and other concomitant social ills result in a lowered intellectual drive (Eichenwald & Fry, 1969; Scrimshaw & Gordon, 1968). To understand the problems of mental retardation in poverty areas we have to adopt a different basis of observation (Kurtz & Wolfensberger, 1969; Wortis, 1970). The child who does not get enough to eat will be a dullard in the classroom regardless of his genetic endowment. The child who has little chance to express himself in acceptable, creative ways outside his own little pocket of experience will be a dullard in the classroom no matter how often he bathes. And the child who emerges from the inner city, overwhelmed by uncontrollable sensory experiences, will be a dullard in the classroom regardless of the length of his hair or the style of his clothing.

The problem of getting enough to eat is not just that of whether the child had a breakfast or will be given a hot lunch; it is not a matter of a specific number of calories taken in on a specific day. Rather it is that of a proper diet over a whole lifetime, including correct nutrition for the mother even before the child's conception (Miller, 1968). Answers to the problem include maternity clinics where mothers can get advice on their diet and physical well-being before conception, so that they learn the things they must do to make themselves proper hosts for their babies (thus increasing the need for early sex education in planning parenthood); a visiting nursing service which sees the newborn babies during the first two weeks of life and follows up with regular visits to mothers of babies who have nutritional or other difficulties; and help for mothers who cannot nurse their children in obtaining special formulas required to offset whatever deficiencies are present.

In general, every effort must be made during the first eight or ten weeks of a child's life to insure the fullest production of deoxyribonucleic acid **(DNA)**, for nutritional deficiencies during this period seem inevitably to produce shortages of DNA and ribonucleic acid **(RNA)** (Dobbing, 1968). DNA is a substance necessary for the passing on of characteristics deemed hereditary; the composition of RNA determines the ability of the body to synthesize proteins, transfer signals throughout the nervous system, maintain the genetic code, and provide information storage.

The problem of creative imagination is another serious one for the children of subcultural communities. The communities themselves have their own organization, patterns of living, and language structure (Baratz, 1969). A child raised in such a community must compete first within it and then within the dominant culture, which may keep him subjugated. As a result he may feel out of place and unwanted outside of his own street or home, with no ability to reach a broader future and no outlet for creative imagination as society would accept the term. Intelligent people may respond to such **frustrations** in violent ways that threaten the peace and quiet of nonpoverty areas, but nonetheless show great creativity. Those of less intelligence also bear the heavy and destructive social burden and as a result are much less apt to develop acceptable adaptation than are their more affluent cousins of similar basic abilities. The answer for both the more and the less intelligent poor is an expansion of preschool experiences for the very young, so that they can learn the feelings of self-pride and personal worth necessary for academic achievement and socially useful, creative behavior.

The problem of cognitive growth and development often leads us to speak of **deprivation,** but we must recognize that it lies in areas other than those usually discussed. A child is not "culturally deprived" because his family does not own books; today the major cultural agent of our times is television, which teaches children to count and to read in a word-recognition sense. Only in the more comfortable areas of society do books take on a special meaning. Here mother or father will read a bedtime story, a child is praised for going to the library, he receives books for birthday or Christmas presents, and so on. But other than this, there does not seem to be a specific relationship between the presence of books and cognitive attainment. When we think of deprivation we must think of something much more profound and insidious.

Cognitive growth and development are basic. A new baby in a comfortably placed family is usually given a corner of his own in the house, where some effort is made to provide quiet and darkness for an appropriate amount of daytime sleep; his parents attempt as much as possible to keep him in a controlled, stable, sanitary environment so that he will have optimal growth and development during this period when his brain is maturing faster than at any other time in his life. But in the homes of the poor, although parents attempt to do the same thing, the accomplishment usually is far from optimal. Houses are crowded, the noise level is high, the different ages of the people using the rooms cause them to be lighted at all hours, the houses are poorly constructed and do not give adequate protection. Polluted air and industrial smells may be added to odors of rancid lard and human smells. The baby may be exposed to vermin, rodents, and other animals. A child developing under such circumstances is by no means deprived of sensory experiences; rather he is drowned in sights, smells, tastes, feels, and noises (Deutsch, 1964; Kessler, 1970).

The child of poverty has relatively few resources that enable him to cope, and what he has may have been dulled by the other poverty factors. As a result, his cognitive growth may be slowed and—unless major efforts are made to reverse the trend—the result will be a child who focusses mainly on survival processes and has relatively low intellectual drive. Such children are not mentally retarded at birth, but they may become retarded and often neurologically damaged by the neglect of society. Since the human organism responds to **remedial** measures if they are applied early enough, a reversal of the dulling effects of poverty can be accomplished by aiding the parent with the kinds of service resources we have described.

Once more we see that the real test of any classification or labeling scheme must be how well it serves the person being labeled. The vital test is its relevance to the treatment, training, and rehabilitation of a specific retarded child. If it tends to keep the necessary services from him it is bad. The services that must be available can be divided conveniently into the three areas of general **clinical services,** educational services, and medical services.

Services Needed: Clinical, Educational, and Medical

Under general clinical services come rehabilitation and therapeutic processes, even though they may not be strictly clinical in the usual sense. They start with the concept that in the behavior of the retarded child there is a variety of elements that should be modified. As an example, the boy who throws a rock through a window is using skills that would be socially approved on a baseball field; the problem is not to get him to stop throwing, but to get him to stop throwing rocks at windows. Such a modification of behavior is not based on the introduction of new skills but rather on an improvement in personal and **social responsibility.** The mentally retarded respond quite readily to such therapeutic interventions, which are capable of reversing some of the behaviors that gave them the original label (Leland & Smith, 1965).

Generally, the material in a retarded child's environment comes pouring in upon him and, unfortunately, also goes pouring out as he fails to identify or utilize the cues. There is not a problem here of receiving stimuli, but rather of differentiating them and of using them. Clinical **intervention** is not based upon testing and diagnosis. Rather, no matter what specific techniques are used, clinical intervention is used to help the child regroup or reorganize his behavior so that he may utilize social cues in order to cope more effectively. There is a difference, at least with the retarded child, between helping him sort out information that he already has and helping him gain new information; the former is clinical intervention, the latter educational intervention.

Educational services help the child gain additional information so that he can create new behavioral patterns. He may be given specific retraining or rehabilitation by use of **behavior modification** techniques such as programmed reading or **precision teaching** or he may be given special education, which provides information or develops skills he has not been able to attain through standard methods. Such education may range from singing simple songs and having social experiences with his peers to telling time, counting money, or reading key words. The aim here is not only to regroup social forces but to provide new information that can be utilized for survival. Both clinical and educational intervention are required if a child is to adapt to his surroundings, but they are considered as separate services because they are provided by specialists who have different kinds of training.

A number of biomedical disorders often are associated with mental retardation, and they require medical services. For instance, while many epileptics are not retarded, many others are; there is evidence that the seizure pattern retards learning in some children (Eyman, Moore, Capes, & Zachotsky, 1970). These children will gain both from clinical and from educational intervention, but medical control of the seizures must come first of all. Similarly, children with certain orthopedic handicaps, certain blind and deaf children, and children who are bedridden and require nursing care have a primary need for medical intervention. Even the more usual retarded child has a group of medical, or at least public-health nursing, needs that should be satisfied; although his top-priority needs may be clinical and educational, such matters as dietary modification and disease protection are also essential.

Services rendered a mentally retarded child should be mainly directed at those aspects of his behavior that have given him the label. Of the five aspects of intelligence —sensory-motor development, **rate of learning** (IQ), cognition, social intelligence, and adaptive behavior—the labeling is based most upon failures in the latter three. Therefore our first concern must be with modifying these aspects.

Let us consider more basically just what we are trying to do, or more precisely, what we *should* be trying to do. If a person is hospitalized for appendicitis, the appendix is the major concern; if the surgeon also finds a congenital but relatively harmless **anomaly,** he still deals with the appendix and in time discharges the patient without great concern for the anomaly and certainly without waiting for it somehow to correct itself. When a retarded person is institutionalized, those aspects of his condition that can be treated are often ignored, and those which cannot be treated are often emphasized. He may be kept in the institution for an indefinite time—waiting, in effect, for his brain to be restored. Even under the best of circumstances patients are often kept in institutions long after they have received maximum benefits; movement back to the community is not a major social objective (Kugel & Wolfensberger, 1969; Ennis & Friedman, 1974). This is partly because in our increasingly technical civilization it is difficult to insure full employment for the able members of society and as a result the mentally retarded come to be thought of as surplus population. We are inclined to forget our responsibility to the less able members. Our real concern with the mentally retarded must be in finding ways to fit them into the total social structure, even though this requires changes in social patterns and changes in the basic value system of society (Farber, 1968).

Thus in a broad perspective we are concerned not so much with who should be considered mentally retarded as we are with how to organize a social base which will let us use the abilities and skills present in all of our citizens. Each retarded individual, whatever the degree of his affliction, has some potential that should be developed. If biomedical or sensory-motor impairments are great, the potential will be less, but most of the people with whom we are dealing do not have impairments so overwhelming that they cannot somehow fit into society. In fact, the question of how to modify or reverse their behavior so that they can fit in may be an important one for the future development of a democratic and a peaceful social order.

The true measure of a civilization is its ability to give each of its citizens the opportunity to live as full and complete a life as possible. All people must be permitted to become contributing citizens. We must also use all necessary resources to prevent the development of mental disabilities and to provide decent conditions in what now are substandard areas.

4

Social Attitudes

Mental retardation is a unique problem, not only because of its nature but also because society approaches it in a manner different from other childhood disorders. Social attitudes toward it are highly stereotyped. Society has an extreme intolerance for difference and seems unable to accept the unusual. In our democratic tradition, people who deviate are permitted to do so if they are not socially dangerous, but society is not always sure whether or not the inferior person is dangerous. As a result, the question of whether he should be permitted to remain in contact with society becomes a major one.

This is not true of all cultures. Dr. Robert Edgerton[1] tells the story that when he was visiting a tribe in Africa, he observed a group in one village that was getting ready for its morning work. Among them he saw a young man lead an old one across the compound. The young man was not doing a very good job, but he was getting the older man, who was blind, from his own hut to the larger conference hut on the far side of the village. Edgerton asked his guide about the scene and was told that the old man was a village elder who had gone blind, but whose wisdom was valued and who still participated in tribal deliberations. The young man was not smart enough to hunt or farm, but he had two good eyes and could lead the older man, if sometimes precariously, to the

[1]Personal communication, Parsons State Hospital and Training Center, Kansas, 1965.

places he needed to go. The young man, though obviously retarded, was a contributing member of that society.

As a culture becomes more complex it has less need for its less proficient members. Thus, in our culture in the days when a thousand hands were needed to harvest a wheat crop, everyone in the community, no matter how poorly he functioned, had a place in the harvest. Today when much of the work is done by machinery, there is no need for that many hands. The less able members of the community are apt merely to get in the way; they perhaps can bring water to the harvesters or do similar minor tasks, but in general the harvest is brought in by a combination of machines and a few men with technical skills. Unlike the society that Edgerton observed, our rural society does not need individuals of low ability to carry out simple tasks. This example illustrates how increased technology laid the basis for the practice of separation. The present public practice of separation and isolation has resulted in an extreme form of dehumanization and depersonalization. This practice is not a necessary part of the treatment of mental retardation and must be changed (Declaration of General and Special Rights, 1969).

IQ Vs. Adaptation

Science has not always helped. The greatest disservice that psychologists have performed in the area of mental retardation has been to emphasize the IQ as an indicator of the condition. There is a major difference between the youngster who achieves a low IQ because of internal biological problems that interfere with his learning (Zigler, 1967), and the one who achieves a low IQ because he is being tested with an instrument that measures areas of learning to which he has not been exposed. Between sixty and eighty percent of all retarded individuals are culturally or environmentally deprived (President's Panel, 1962), a situation quite different from other causes of mental retardation. The result may be similar in terms of the child's inability to meet school or community standards (Girardeau, 1968), but the deprived child often can function quite well in his own environment while the retarded child cannot (President's Committee, 1970).

One certainly should not say that a child who is completely familiar with all of the back alleys of his neighborhood, who if he is running away knows how to get from one place to another without getting caught, and who is able to move freely at will in areas requiring an advanced degree of coordination in climbing and jumping, is functioning at a retarded level. His proficiency in survival skills is far greater than that of the more comfortably placed child, but he has not learned the same things as the other child and when he is faced with an IQ test it almost literally is in a foreign language (Baratz, 1969).

When one goes into a deprived area one finds a number of very bright children who have a high degree of gang leadership and who are extremely knowing about the things that go on in their environment, often much more so than those of the same age outside the area. Because of this fact, ghetto children may shock outsiders. A normal five-year-old in the ghetto knows more about sexual activity and can use more four-letter words than his better-off counterpart. Children of this type have learned a way of life that is necessary if they are to survive; it is true that they may be insensitive and even as adults may be callous to the needs and feelings of their own associates (Fanon, 1968), but they obviously have learned very well in a way no mentally retarded child could achieve.

But in the same deprived areas there are children who do not learn in this manner and who have become visible because of their inabilities. They are not aware of the things around them, are not mobile, and are hyperdependent; such normal needs as dressing and toileting have to be provided for them. They do not have language facility even in terms of their own subcommunity, and they cannot survive without a great deal of help. Such children can truly be described as mentally retarded. Yet their IQ's may not be much lower than those of the able children who can survive easily (Heber, 1968; Lamp & Yater, 1968); the IQ test is simply not appropriate for either kind of child.

Is Retardation Inherited?

The history of genetics in our culture has also had an unfortunate effect upon our concepts of retardation. Based on Aristotelian thinking, for over a thousand years we have had the idea of "human nature," a certain basic, specific way in which an organism was supposed to perform. Aristotle believed that if an organism did not perform in a manner consistent with its nature, it had been invaded by a demon that was making it do things contrary to its nature. This concept was carried down to the Middle Ages, and even at the end of them we find Martin Luther telling us:

> Eight years ago, there was one at Dessau whom I, Martinus Luther, saw and grappled with. He was twelve years old, had the use of his eyes and all his senses, so that one might think he was a normal child. But he did nothing but gorge himself as much as four peasants or threshers. He ate, defecated and drooled and, if anyone tackled him, he screamed. If things didn't go well, he wept. So I said to the Prince of Anhalt; "If I were the Prince, I should take this child to the Moldau River which flows near Dessau and drown him." But the Prince of Anhalt and the Prince of Saxony, who happened to be present, refused to follow my advice. Thereupon I said: "Well, then the Christians shall order the Lord's Prayer to be said in church and pray that the dear Lord take the Devil away." This was done daily in Dessau and the changeling died in the following year. When Luther was asked why he had made such a recommendation, he replied that he was firmly of the opinion that such changelings were merely a mass of flesh, a *massa carnis,* with no soul. For it is in the Devil's power that he corrupts people who have reason and souls when he possesses them. The Devil sits in such changelings where their soul should have been! (Luther, 1652, in Kanner, 1964, p. 7)

Although the first geneticists did not believe in possession by demons, they were strongly influenced by Aristotelian thought and they believed in an unchangeable gene that carried the qualities of man's nature. Just as early the demon was to be destroyed, now "wrong" genes should be destroyed, a concept still sometimes found in eugenics. Yet modern research has demonstrated that variations within the gene pool lead to a healthier, stronger species; the elements suspected of having created retardation might well be related to lack of such variations. The notion of a single genetic pattern being best thus becomes destructive to the species rather than beneficial (Dobzhansky, 1967).

A long-standing social stereotype has it that retardation is mainly inherited (Burt, 1966). There was for many years a tendency for "better" families to deny the existence among them of retarded individuals. A long history exists of people being hidden away in attics or sent to private living situations in the hope that they would die and the public would never know that they had existed (White, 1969). The assumption was that nothing could be done for such a child, and that since retardation was inherited his existence would indicate to others that the family was deficient and thus damage their success in business or social activities. The poorer elements of society were not affected by these biases; there was another stereotype that poverty was inherited and that the poor had many abnormal genes which they passed on through immoral and improper breeding (Goddard, 1912).

A logical development of this idea was the workhouse, such as the one described by Dickens in *Oliver Twist,* where poverty-stricken, illegitimate youngsters were cared for in the most miserable way because—according to then-current thought—they were really young animals and therefore deserved no better. Many of our institutions in the United States were based on this workhouse concept. The State of Indiana, for example, organized Muscatatuck State School as an experimental farm colony to demonstrate the most up-to-date farming techniques, with retarded patients to do the work. There was no thought that they would ever leave the institution; they simply provided the labor with no recompense. It was not until the late 50's that this philosophy was abandoned there.[2]

[2]The senior author was Chief Psychologist at Muscatatuck State School, Indiana, from 1954 to 1957.

As we begin to recognize that inheritance is not the fixed, inflexible matter we once thought it and that **chromosomal errors** are not necessarily transmittable and may be correctable, and as we also recognize that environmental factors may have a strong influence on retardation, the ability to change behavior becomes paramount. Until recently we have had the notion that whatever is done to a retarded person or whatever kind of institution he is placed in must be directed at "curing" him, and he was institutionalized either to protect society or to be "cured." But mental retardation is not a disease, and in our present state of science we probably cannot reverse most of the contributing biomedical factors anyway. Modification of behavior must be our aim.

"At Least He Can Be Happy"

There has been a humane concept that the main thing to achieve for the retarded is happiness. Since you cannot do anything else for him, so the argument goes, "at least he can be happy." But as we perhaps *can* do something for him, we must raise the question of whether happiness is necessarily the right goal. There are serious difficulties in defining happiness, but one common supposition is that it exists in completely hedonistic social surroundings; yet there is research which demonstrates that patients become dissatisfied in just such environments (Cleland & Swartz, 1969). Whatever else the vague thing called happiness may be, it seems to be a byproduct of relatively effective social functioning. And so in practice we must be more concerned with the problem of where the child is going than how happy he is; we have a responsibility in this regard both to him as a person and to society as a whole.

Programs built on the concept of rehabilitation, behavior modification, or the development of adaptive skills must center around the notions that each retarded person has someplace to go, that some aspect of his behavior is reversible, that he is just as apt to become emotionally disturbed as other children, and that intensive programs of dependency-creating, dehumanizing service such as the typical "tender, loving care" **(TLC)** can stultify him. He should be institutionalized only if he has profound biomedical problems or if his behavior is such that he cannot survive in his community (Shellhaas & Nihira, 1969; 1970); the second reason is by far the more frequent one.

The child separated from his community for medical reasons should receive medical care. The child who has been separated for behavioral reasons should receive treatment and training to modify his behavior. In either case, when the treatment or training has been completed he should be returned to his home. We should not, as has been done in the past, set up criteria which in many instances cannot be met by even normal members of the community and then state that the individual who cannot meet them must stay in the institution; and we should not say that treatment or training is unfeasible because of the level of his retardation.

Every Child Can Be Helped

As the result of this latter assertion, some of the more modern, well-maintained children's hospitals and institutions contain wards of children (who have a variety of **etiological** and behavioral diagnoses) who receive no treatment, who rarely are given modification programs; and who vegetate emotionally and psychologically, even though they receive first-rate attention as far as their physical and medical needs are concerned. Such wards often have pictures, toys, and music and the bleak atmosphere of yesteryear has been dissipated. The patients are often gentled, and in a broad sense the campaigns for more humane treatment of the retarded individual have left their marks and other major efforts to create "happy" patients go forward. But the child has everything done for him, he is given no opportunity to make any kinds of decisions, there are no systematic goals established for improvement in adaptive behavior or modification of current behavior, and in general he has no opportunity to develop elementary maturational processes. In short, these children have been written off psychologically in spite of an increasing body of evidence that modification is possible and that every child, regardless of how retarded he may be, can be helped in some manner (Leland & Goldberg, 1957).

Only those people whose treatment and training needs are beyond our current range of knowledge should remain institutionalized, and then only until our knowledge catches up with their needs. Wherever possible we should treat and train children in local facilities that can provide the necessary services without also having to function as hotels; we now have a large body of knowledge concerning possible ways of treating and training retarded individuals, and most often there are ways to help them that do not require that they be isolated from society.

Thus institutional standards must begin to reflect respect for the patient (Declaration of General and Special Rights, 1969) and include the concept that the child will leave the facility as rapidly as possible if the staff carries out its responsibilities to him. Our basic philosophy must be that each person must be helped, to the fullest extent of our ability, to become equipped for a contributing role in society. This is not a matter of bringing him to a normal level of intelligence, but rather of helping him develop a level of adaptive behavior that will permit him either to be returned to his community or transferred to a local facility near it.

Other stereotypes about inheritance have led to difficulties for the retarded child. Imperfect genes were supposed, by definition, to be transmitters of negative characteristics and thus dangerous. The recent controversy on criminality is a current example of this (Price & Whatmore, 1967a, 1967b; McWhirter, 1969). The evil person, the delinquent person, the criminal, were thought to have inherited their characteristics and this inheritance was associated with the same genetic error as retardation. The earlier geneological studies ignored environmental circumstances such as malnutrition, disease, educational deprivation, and cultural **disadvantages** (Goddard, 1912). This concept of a feeble-minded criminal type has been scientifically discredited, but it still crops up (Haller, 1963), especially in rumor and in the sensational press.

Retardation and Sexual Activity

Another stereotype of long standing associates retardation with abnormal sexual activity and prowess. One major reason for institutionalizing young females has been the assumption that they might become promiscuous (Shellhaas & Nihira, 1969), and the idea of an over-endowed feebleminded male goes back at least to the Georgian novel, *Fanny Hill* (Cleland [1749], 1963). No doubt some retarded girls are promiscuous and some retarded boys lack sexual inhibitions, but more typically, the retarded lack sexual energy and the more retarded they are the more apt they are to be completely impotent (Mosier, Grossman, & Dingman, 1965). The exceptions are usually those who are environmentally deprived rather than biologically retarded or those whose sexual behavior falls into the accepted patterns of their subcultures and is unrelated to defective intellectual processes.

Very rarely, as in Klinefelter's Syndrome (Klinefelter, Reisenstein, & Albright, 1942), genetic **errors** produce a clearly degenerative sexual process (Jacobs & Strong, 1959). Such conditions are much less frequent than are pathological forms of sexual behavior in emotionally disturbed people of apparently normal genetic organization; those who are guilty of sadistic behavior, gang rapes, or other clearly antisocial sexual acts are almost always individuals of normal or even superior intelligence. From a criminal's viewpoint the mentally retarded are probably the worst people to include in any organized crime, for they do not know when to run, where to go, or how to proceed without exposing other members of the gang. Despite the stereotypes, the retarded member of society is not usually the delinquent.

Diagnostic Processes

All of these stereotypes represent what mental retardation is *not*. We now must look at what it is and how it is diagnosed. As a starting point there is the AAMD definition which was given earlier, a definition that includes the elements of subaverage intellectual functioning, occurrence during the developmental period, and deficit in adaptive behavior (Heber, 1961; Grossman, 1973).

One of the first questions asked under the traditional approach is how to differentiate mentally retarded behavior and emotionally disturbed behavior. Some of the older definitions tried to explain the difference by using the idea of **pseudo-retardation,** saying that for a child to be mentally retarded he must have types of behavior that were "incurable" (Doll, 1941). If the child was capable of being cured—or if the types of behavior were capable of being modified—he was only a pseudo-retardate and was probably really emotionally disturbed. But this explanation led to many undesirable results. It implied on the one hand that anyone who could be helped was not actually retarded, and on the other that a truly retarded person could not be helped. Because it suggested that retarded behavior was caused by problems such as emotional disturbance, children often did not receive the kind of help they needed; parents thought that since they were emotionally disturbed rather than *retarded* they should have no problems in learning or cognition, and sometimes even felt that they failed to learn because they were "bad" or "spoiled."

The concept of pseudo-retardation had one other bad aspect: it depended on something happening. The child had to demonstrate that the behavior was reversible or "curable" before he was considered a pseudo-retardate. This set up a paradoxical situation in which there was no point in trying to help a truly retarded child because he was by definition incurable, yet until someone tried to help him and did manage to reverse some of his behavior he could not be classified as a pseudo-retardate. Thus only those children who by accident received help or were somehow able to correct themselves and thus apparently "outgrew" their problems could be classified as pseudo-retardates. The result was a completely spurious definition (Bialer, 1969).

Inherent in the concept of pseudo-retardates vs. retardates was the assumption that an individual had to be one thing or the other. He had to be mentally retarded *or* emotionally disturbed, but never some combination of the two. This idea of **differential diagnosis**—that a subject's problems arose either all in one area or all in the other—created impossible diagnostic boundaries. In fact, a retarded child can be phobic, a **schizophrenic** child can be retarded, or a **brain-damaged** child can be emotionally disturbed. There are no tests or validated behavioral signs or other approaches that reveal whether a child is functioning at a retarded level because of an emotional disturbance or because of a "true" retardation (Bialer, 1969).

In arriving at a psychological diagnosis we first consider the **case history** to learn what kinds of behavior brought the child to the clinic. Then we observe on-going behavior in the clinic, using both standardized **psychometric** instruments and various forms of free observation in a variety of settings (Leland & Smith, 1965, Chap. 9). Next we make other observations drawn from reports of other disciplines—medical reports, for example—and take measures of adaptive behavior, perceptual motor performance, vision, hearing, or the like, depending upon what is necessary to supplement and perhaps explain the performance already noted. Finally, the information thus derived is compared with child development expectations for children of that age and cultural group, corrected for any specific environmental differences. If it then appears that the child functions in a consistent pattern noticeably different from the norm, we say that a diagnostic entity exists.

A child rarely presents a unified set of symptoms or behaviors throughout all four of the steps. More typically, the symptoms indicate a combination of diagnostic entities. These have been approached either on the basis of **syndromes** (American Psychiatric Association, 1968) or etiologies (Heber, 1961). Neither of these approaches stands alone, and we may have an individual who could be described as mentally retarded, **organic, neurotic,** and/or **psychotic** (Beier, 1964). There is no reason to suppose that if he is diagnosed as mentally deficient this eliminates the possibility of emotional disturbance or psychological disorder, as once was thought. On the contrary, a combination of such factors is the most typical condition.

One other factor, that of **social neglect,** must be considered in diagnosis. There is, as we have seen, a high risk that impoverished children will be retarded because of educational neglect and poor environment; but despite the odds, most of them are not. However, if in addition there are possible genetic factors working against a child, the probability becomes higher that he will be retarded. And if one adds social neglect, the odds against the child become greater yet, even though at birth there may not have been any specific biomedical signs of retardation. Social neglect, which must be considered different from "maternal deprivation," is apt to become critical with ghetto children at about age three. Up to that point the child is loved and gentled and given more personal attention than his richer counterpart, but thereafter he is treated not as a baby but as a young person, and he is more likely to be slapped or even beaten than petted and loved. Suddenly he must adapt to a new situation. As a result he will mature faster than the child outside the ghetto, but he is less apt to learn to use his imagination by being exposed to fairy tales or imaginative games. He may get some of these things through television, but the passive experience of watching imaginative material is not a good substitute for active participation in it; there seems to be a lowering of the learning curve when children let television do their thinking for them.

Thus children already in the high-risk group are exactly those whose learning potential is lowered by social neglect. When this happens there is a high probability the child will emerge as a retarded individual. This type of retardation is completely a product of our social attitudes, for under better social conditions it would not occur. Since all socially neglected children do not become retarded, we must emphasize the combination of factors. Those factors which can be modified most quickly and easily are exactly those causing high risk: malnutrition, poor disease control, destructive social ecology. One approach to the problem would be a system of family allotments coupled with neighborhood resource centers. Overall, the answer lies in prevention much more than in correction.

Once the diagnostic entities are established, the next step begins. It is to assemble clues as to the interpersonal relationships and coping strategies that the child has developed. Instead of searching for causes at this point, it is better to learn the ways in which the child attempts to deal with social pressures and frustrations. For example, a child who has not in his eight years learned those things expected of a typical eight-year-old probably will have developed certain kinds of defensive behavior. If he regularly has been asked questions that he cannot answer, he may well have a negative, suspicious reaction to any questions, based on a thoroughly realistic knowledge that he is going to be asked things to which he cannot respond. If the examiner understands this orientation he will more readily understand the reasons for some of the behavior that has been observed and thus will arrive sooner at an analysis of the basic problems. Knowledge of the way the child meets situations will help to establish the corrective measures that must be taken first, and this in turn will demonstrate the basic areas of deficiency. Once we know these basic areas we can study the child's coping resources more accurately; further careful observation of the severely retarded may, for example, reveal coping strategies typical of emotional disturbance—as in the case of some metabolic disorders (Leland, 1957).

Labels Are Not Enough

It adds little to our knowledge simply to give the child a label. If we say that he has a low IQ or even give the IQ number we say nothing about what must be done for his condition. If we say that he is neurotic, organic, or psychotic we say nothing about the treatment or training that he must have. A diagnosis to serve the child must reveal the behavioral areas that actually are deficient; we must start with the problem that needs correcting and use the best available information as a basis for the correction (Leland, 1969a).

Society, with its fear of the unknown, has demanded labels. It has then acted upon them, sometimes almost ignoring the people who carry them. But as approaches to diagnoses based on the relationship between societal needs and what the person does begin to provide a basis for change, social attitudes based on fear or disappointment should also change, and as a result those labels which do not provide information can be discarded.

5

Minimal Brain Dysfunction

There is a small group of children whose behavior has been the subject of confused diagnostic efforts because the established categories overlapped and verification of the exact condition could be established only by autopsy. This group has been described as "mentally deficient" or "organic" with long lists of symptoms reminiscent of the Fourier Syndrome (Mackinnon, 1944). The only thing on which all investigators have agreed is that these children cannot adapt properly and present learning difficulties (Birch, 1964).

This group of children often has highly visible behavior, not because of early developmental impairment but because of what usually are known as **learning disorders.** Most behavior is part of a learning process, and thus any disorder in behavior might be called a learning disorder; but the term normally is applied to a lack of ability to respond acceptably to academic matters—the "processes of speech, language, perception, behavior, reading, spelling, or arithmetic" (Kirk, 1966). An alternative term is "learning disability" (*Journal of Learning Disabilities*).

The first sign of this type of maladaptation generally occurs in school. The child may have had a somewhat chaotic home adjustment, but the parents usually have assumed that once he gets to school everything will be all right. However, when he finally is in school the full problem emerges, and he is unable to respond acceptably to demands for specific learning.

Such a child will have inappropriate social responses, or behavior problems and learning disabilities, or school problems or some combination of these factors. The treatment of one problem will not necessarily solve the others. Diagnosis must include comparisons of levels of functioning, detailed behavioral descriptions, and correlations of the disability with expected performance and child development patterns; the remedies must emerge from the diagnostic information (Bateman, 1964). The aim of our remedies should be modification of the undesirable behavior so that the child will be able to fit adequately into social and adademic situations.

As we discuss problem-solving goals we must be concerned with descriptive accuracy. The labels of "organic" or "brain damage" do great harm unless the individuals so labeled receive services specific to their difficulties; no better purpose is served by attributing their behavior to lack of motivation or general alienation. Rather, the specific behaviors to be reversed must be clarified.

Clarification of Behaviors

Clinical entities are collections of physical features and behaviors. Symptoms do not exist by themselves, but are parts of larger groups of manifestations. Both the whole and the parts must be understood for effective modification. A record of school failure must be approached in the same way. Children often have learning disorders as a result of **minimal brain dysfunctions;** their brain damage is too slight to provide clear-cut neurological entities, but is enough to cause learning irregularities that make them highly visible (Jabbour, 1968). Minimal brain dysfunction has been defined as referring to children of "near-average, average, or above-average general intelligence with certain learning or behavioral disabilities ranging from mild to severe, which are associated with deviations of function of the central nervous system" (Clements, 1966, p. 9).

The weakness in this definition is the use of "average general intelligence," a concept usually based on IQ. Just as low IQ's do not necessarily indicate retarded functioning, IQ's in the normal range do not necessarily indicate average functioning. A diagnosis, if it is to be anything more than a label, must be based on a combination of observed behavior and clinical findings. Children diagnosed with minimal brain dysfunction often present a behavioral and clinical picture similar to that of most educationally retarded children, and they benefit from the programs that we advocate for them.

Such children, although they are not brain-damaged in the usual sense, have many of the symptoms of brain damage such as **hyperactivity** or poor concentration (Knights & Hinton, 1967). These symptoms also include poor coordination; such a child is typically the last one on his block to learn to ride a tricycle or to use roller skates. He also seems to suffer from a **hypersensitivity** to sensory input, so that he is overly aware of extraneous sounds or movements: each sound, movement, or smell sets off its own demand for a response and a chaos of stimuli results. This is not because the child fails to differentiate, but because he cannot respond to all of them at the same time and yet is unable to establish priorities. The result may be typical frustrated behavior—tantrums, screaming, and striking out—although he is in fact seeking peace and quiet rather than the usual rewards sought by such behavior. The child may not react at all to his mother's refusal to give him a cookie, but may have an uncontrollable tantrum because there is a bird chirping outside his window.

The inability of the child to settle into one specific activity or to organize his time often makes his home adjustment difficult and as a result his parents may encourage him to spend a great deal of his time out of doors. This leads to a diagnostic pattern described as the "over-tanned, cleft-chin syndrome." The child is over-tanned because he spends so much time out of doors and his damaged chin, nose, or forehead results from the combination of his insatiable need to explore and his poor coordination; he is constantly climbing trees or fences and is constantly falling from them. Clinicians have come to recognize that when they are faced with a hyperactive, highly-tanned child who has scars on his face but is otherwise normal in appearance, they probably are dealing with a child who has minimal dysfunction.

One of the main difficulties of these children is that they do not gain insight from the things that happen to them. They may repeat the same ineffective behavior over and over again (Bender, 1949). As a result they will build up an accumulation of failures, which, accompanied by criticism and punishment from parents and teachers, adds to the level of personal frustration. Classmates or **siblings** quickly realize that such children cannot control their outbursts and purposely tap on the table or do other things that make the child explode and probably cause him to be punished, thus creating an entertaining diversion. The victims soon develop a general feeling of persecution and lack of worth.

Some of these children are constantly on the move, but others are not; hyperactivity need not be present. Most of them are hypersensitive, however, to the total stimuli of their environment (Kinsbourne, 1970). The child may sit for hours in front of the television set—which represents peace for him because someone else is carrying out the movement and he does not have to worry about it but just let it happen—and cause no problems. Then if a sibling comes in and makes a remark or a noise, the quiet child may turn into a highly and noisily frustrated child. And often his parents will not want him to sit in front of television indefinitely; he may, for example, have homework to do, and on being told to do the homework he probably will respond in the same disrupted manner.

Then if he does not understand parts of the homework because he could not concentrate on them in class he will be additionally frustrated. If his parents criticize or punish him for not doing the homework he probably will feel that he is being punished for not understanding, and will consider himself unjustly treated and by implication disliked. The result may be symptoms of a behavioral disorder and a condition that may be described as emotional disturbance (Thomas, Chess, & Birch, 1968). His only calmness or quiet is derived from activities which provide an escape when someone or something else is responsible for the movement and he can concentrate on it. He may not know what he is watching, but he is able to direct his attention to it and get some peace by not being involved.

The Child in the Classroom

When this child goes to school he is expected to attend specifically to the teacher at all times. But because other activities to which he is so sensitive surround him he cannot always attend only to her, and even when he does there is the further demand that he understand what she is saying or what the classroom activity is about. He must know what is happening; yet he cannot find out what is going on unless he receives highly individualized attention. The general tendency for such a child in such a situation is to block off from his consciousness as much of the classroom as he can, including particularly the teacher, who is the most intrusive element. He then appears to be daydreaming. His lack of coordination makes it difficult for him to function in writing or drawing, with musical instruments, or in other organized activities, as well as at recess, and so school becomes one vast disaster.

Such a child is often considered retarded and is given special tests and evaluations that usually show that his intelligence is within the normal range during the one-to-one interaction with the school psychologist or counsellor. He then is sent back to the classroom, and the teacher begins to suspect that he is lazy, spoiled, bad, or simply not trying hard enough. She probably feels that he is more in need of punishment than special help, which makes life even more difficult for him, and she and other school authorities may even assume that he is incorrigible and should be dropped from school.

Peer Problems

A child of this type usually will be unpopular with his peers. He tends to do or say the wrong thing and he becomes subject to derision. He is easily teased (Knights & Hinton, 1967) and frequently responds with hostility, but his hostile actions are probably ineffective and lead only to more teasing and jeering. Further, because his basic problem leads him to overreact in emotional situations he may explode into uncontrollable fits of anger and aggression, which simply increase the teasing. Any other child who might wish to be friendly will find that he cannot do so and retain his status with the rest of the class. The classroom leaders do not accept the dysfunctioning child and tend to maintain their leadership by taunting him; the main body of the class follow along simply to be part of the group; and the least popular members also join in, thus helping to concentrate the group's derision on someone other than themselves.

A teacher's attitude will help to set the attitudes of the class, a phenomenon also noted with the disadvantaged (Rosenthal & Jacobson, 1968). If, for example, she normally writes on the chalkboard the names of children who daydream or do not get their work done, the child who has learning disorders will find his name on the board almost every day. Other members of the class will be quick to see this and it will reinforce their idea that there is something wrong with him and cause them to ridicule him in the classroom as well as on the playground. There will be no place in school where he is safe and he will be even more likely to react with an emotional outburst, which may cause him to be sent to the principal or otherwise punished.

On the other hand, if the teacher can take time to give such a child individual attention he will often grasp the necessary ideas rapidly and settle down willingly to do his work. Unfortunately this usually must be after school, and so in effect it becomes a punishment for both teacher and child. The parents of a child with these problems must work closely with the teacher. When special programs are not available, it is the family who will need to provide the one-to-one interaction that the child must have. Problems often arise, however, because the child comes to school with forms of behavior that first evolved in the home, and usually the parents have developed strong attitudes toward him, often feeling that he is simply "bad" and that if they must undertake part of the teaching role they are themselves being punished (Snyder & Worden, 1969; Stahlecker, 1965).

Even where such parental reactions do not occur, there are difficulties. If the parents work out methods of continuing his school learning at home, they increase the pressure on the child; if they try to control some of his maladaptive behavior he begins to feel that he cannot do anything right. One of the things that he needs desperately is a "safe harbor," and the attempts to take corrective action at home tend to destroy his last refuge.

Special Programs

The answer appears to lie in various types of special programs for such children. These programs may involve teacher aides (Von Haden & King, 1974), who can work during school hours on a one-to-one basis with children who have learning disorders and can make sure they understand assignments, maintain work patterns, and learn how to establish priorities. An aide should not devote her entire time to these children—they should not be singled out as having their own teacher—but should make spot checks while the classroom teacher is presenting material to the entire class. The use of teaching machines is particularly advantageous for such children (Blackman & Capobianco, 1965), for they provide clearly established goals on a one-to-one basis. The child feels less as though he were under attack, because the machine lets him correct errors on the spot, often before anyone else knows about them. His personally rewarding experience from the impersonal machine lets him evaluate himself and his relationship to his peers. And he leaves the machines behind when he leaves school and is not forced into an additional school situation at home.

All classrooms are not able to have teacher aides or teaching machines. The equipment is often too expensive, and sometimes a classroom would have to be remodeled. Some educational gains may be made through a pattern of individual instruction in a normal classroom setting. One of the main criteria for classroom change is the level of language development; the more verbal child can benefit more directly from personal but standard teaching methods (McCarthy & McCarthy, 1969).

Various other special materials and curricula have been developed for children with these difficulties. One example is the Frostig program (Frostig & Horne, 1964, 1965; Frostig,

1970), which provides special materials that let the child learn the regular subjects in a different way. Elementary classrooms today usually have different groups working in various activities, and so the child with the special material need not be singled out in the eyes of his classmates (Weber, 1970).

Once any of these special programs are established, the teachers usually will respond more positively to the afflicted children, for there will be clear-cut goals for them. And the teachers can see and guide their progress more readily and will have fewer feelings of guilt or frustration because they cannot help them.

Whatever the school situation, parents can help at home by pointing out specific cues to which the child should respond, so that he can learn to isolate the right ones and react properly to them (Zaporozhets, 1960). Usually he will be responsive and grateful for the help, although initially his accumulated frustrations may lead to virtual warfare. But once he is on the right path he will be happy, willing to cooperate, and quite a nice person. Basically, the child must develop a workable level of personal adjustment, so that he knows when he can handle situations by himself and when he must ask for help. The younger he is, the more difficult it is for him to make these decisions; therefore with younger children the emphasis should be upon providing a safe harbor at home. At the same time parents can help the young child by assuring that he has *something* each school day that will establish him as a success. The thing can be, for example, a unique object for "show and tell" or a pertinent news item on the school topic of the week. A routine family activity such as a shopping trip to a neighborhood store can be turned into an excursion from which the child brings away a special or different item to show his class. As the child grows older, more emphasis must be placed on academic work, but if the proper steps have been taken at the younger age he will be able to adjust and will begin, through increased powers of rote memory, to find rewards in specific areas, such as a grade of 100 in spelling.

If, through the help of parents and school, the child's classroom relationships improve, his relationships with his peers and his overall personal adjustment also will tend to improve. If he can learn to seek out adult aid to explain the rules of a game or other activity, he can take part in clubs and similar group efforts and may gradually reach the same level of achievement as his peers. Each step of the way, in each new activity, he will need a period of personal interaction with someone who can give him specific help until he becomes self-adequate enough to know how to handle the situation. Those who help him should do so on the premise that they are dealing with a disorganized brain function and that the basic learning potential is there if the child can learn to give the right priorities to the cues he receives (Levi, 1965).

The function of the professional psychologist in the situation is first of all to give the child a fairly clear-cut idea of the difficulty and the kinds of solutions that are required. Once the problem is explained and defined the child usually will comprehend it in time and will be able to develop his responses with more insight. Comprehension may not occur until he approaches adolescence, but if he has been hearing explanations in various contexts throughout his school years, he will eventually grasp what they involve. The second and probably more important function of the professional is to explain the situation to the child's teachers and parents, who will work with him on a daily basis, and to prepare them to guide and help him.

The prognosis for a child suffering from minimal brain dysfunction is usually good. If the condition can be identified and the child can be helped to develop both an understanding of his problem and a battery of successful coping strategies, he could emerge from adolescence without visible evidence of a learning disorder.[1]

[1]A major review of the research and data surrounding this syndrome can be found in Chalfant and Scheffelin (1969). They have divided the problem into questions of auditory, visual, and haptic transmission; analysis, integration, and storage by the brain; and feedback from behavioral responses. They cite over 600 references and studies. The National Project on Learning Disabilities in Children has prepared a review of the essential questions related to educational, medical, and health services for children with minimal brain dysfunctions (Neurological and Sensory Disease Control Program, 1969). Frostig (1970) discusses the physician's role as it relates to the child's training needs.

6

Defects, Disabilities, and Learning

While the child with minimal dysfunction may be difficult to recognize because of the lack of outward physical signs, there are developmental considerations which mark some children as possibly **"brain injured"** (Ernhart, Graham, Eichman, Marshall, & Thurston, 1963; Graham, Ernhart, Craft, & Berman, 1963) if only through their medical histories. Also, there are some children who might be said to have specific dysfunctions or diagnosable brain damage. The damage may be slight in an anatomical sense but nonetheless, it may be sufficiently evident to be considered the basis of severe learning problems. The extent of the damage or the pattern of the syndrome cannot always be the basis for predicting the extent of the learning disability. However, one can use a sort of axiom that, while all individuals with diagnosable brain damage are not necessarily mentally retarded, the damage will have some measurable effect on the way in which their intellectual processes develop.

Intellectual processes, for the purposes of this book, have been described in terms of sensory-motor development, cognition, adaptive behavior, rate of learning, and social awareness. Impairment in any one of these areas, or any combination of these areas, results in an intellectual process different than the "normal." The child may, because of the specific nature of his impairment, still have an IQ within the normal range, but the broad aspects of his intellectual functioning will still be sufficiently different to make him visible. When this impairment can be directly attributed to an **agenesis** (failure of the brain to grow properly), a **dysgenesis** (failure of the brain to grow along expected lines), or chemical malfunction of the brain, the individual can be described as "brain damaged" or "brain injured."

Brain Damage: Strauss Syndrome

Among children with brain injury are those who exhibit the "Strauss Syndrome." Although Strauss and his co-workers first intended to outline a general pattern of behavior for all brain-damaged children (Strauss & Lehtinen, 1947), they actually described one of several patterns caused by dysfunction, but a large number of the children who do have brain injuries manifest these specific symptoms. Among the symptoms are hyperactivity which causes the child to be "driven," to move constantly from place to place and to change his attention constantly from subject to subject; it is a more intense form of the hyperactivity often seen in children who have minimal dysfunctions. Unlike the child with a minimal dysfunction, however, the one described by Strauss will not be completely disrupted when, for example, somebody moves his foot; but he will concentrate on the moving foot, then perhaps on a singing bird, and then on a reflection of light. The result is a failure to concentrate actually on any one thing, with a pattern of "grasshopper jumps" from stimulus to stimulus.

The jumpy pattern leads to the old clinical educational diagnosis of a short attention span, which means that the child can attend but cannot hold his attention (Fisher, 1970). The jumps often are accentuated by boredom in the classroom (Gordon, 1970); the combination of hyperactivity and short attention span may make it impossible for the teacher to reach the child by traditional methods. If an immediate response is expected from him, the child either will be simply blank (a condition described by later workers than Strauss as **cognitive impotency**) or will make a response that may have been successful in an earlier situation but that is irrelevant in the present one **(perseveration)**.

Another symptom of the Strauss Syndrome was first called hypertension, a good descriptive term but one that now is used instead in connection with heart disease. What was meant was that the child is constantly on edge, is extremely excitable, and has uncontrolled responses. If a situation calls for a mild shout he may respond with a tremendous scream, or if it requires a small movement of the hand, he may make a wild swing of his arm. This all-or-none type of behavior permits no mediation processes.

The child described by Strauss is usually within the normal IQ range or at least on the borderline of normal intelligence, and he will be quite aware of what is going on. Thus he usually realizes his inability to control, and because he knows that he probably will respond incorrectly he resents situations that force him to respond. As a result he may be highly irritable and have a "don't annoy me" attitude. He is able to gain apparent control if he can withdraw from his surroundings into himself, and under these circumstances may be able to hold his attention on some things—for example, television programs—for a considerable time. If he is interrupted, his irritable response is legitimate in the sense that the intrusion violates his own efforts at control; but because the irritability itself tends to be uncontrolled, the results are far more extreme than the intrusion would seem to warrant.

Perseveration—the carrying on of physical or social behavior until it becomes out of place or meaningless—is particularly typical of such a child. Thus Bender (1938) describes a brain-damaged child who, once he began to whirl, would continue to spin until he was stopped. Or a child may repeat speech phrases because he seems to like the sound of the words. This sort of behavior is found in normal young children, but it tends to continue in brain-damaged children well past the age when normal children drop it. A number of tests (Bender, 1938; Graham & Kendall, 1960; *Lincoln-Oseretsky,* 1955; Witkin, 1950) have been developed that bring out the various reactions typical of the syndrome; diagnosis of it is relatively simple, but the major problem with children who suffer from it is how they can be trained.

One proposal has been that the child be taken by himself into a room with gray walls, without windows, and with no pictures, lights, noises, or other distractions to draw his attention from his desk or booth (Strauss & Kephart, 1955). This probably is an effective way to teach specific information to a child with brain damage—or to one without it (Browning, 1967; Browning & Shaver, 1970). But this procedure in no way prepares the child to function amidst the distractions of normal society. In fact, if he is conditioned to learn in such highly controlled surroundings he will have even greater difficulty coping when he returns to his normal community environment.

A more effective approach is to train such children in a regular classroom, but to limit the number of cues presented at one time by the use of individual booths within the room (Haring & Phillips, 1962). The classroom can be a normal one, with windows, lights, pictures, sounds, and other children, but the booth gives the brain-damaged child a place where he can retreat from distractions and go into a specific learning posture. Teaching machines are helpful for these children just as they are for those with minimal dysfunctions, and the booths may contain such machines; when the machine rewards the child for having achieved certain goals, he can regard this as permission to return again to the class and interact with them until the next learning need faces him. The arrangement that provides both isolation in booths and socialization in the classroom will let him discover for himself what he needs to do personally when he has specific things to learn and, on the other hand, how he can interact with his peers.

If the child is hyperactive, he should be given legitimate ways to express this feature of the syndrome; he can be asked to clean chalkboards, run errands, or even do forms of busywork devised by the teacher. This approach should continue until the excess activity can be brought under control by treatment and training (Doubros & Daniels, 1966). The child may also be able to concentrate and learn better if instead of sitting at his desk he can stand beside it or walk around it. He should not, however, be permitted entirely to leave the desk without the teacher's permission, or to roam constantly around the room, things that he may tend to do if he is left totally to his own impulses.

The mission of a psychologist with children who demonstrate the Strauss Syndrome is similar to his mission with those who have minimal dysfunctions. He should explain the situation to the child, but his more important work is in **counseling** parents and teachers as to how they can work out methods of using the more difficult aspects of the child's behavior—for example, the hyperactivity and the jumpy attention—as part of the teaching situation, and as to how they can help him develop control strategies as he grows older.

The handicap of such a child probably will be relatively permanent; he is not likely to outgrow it in the usual sense, but it can become part of his learning apparatus if he can understand it and if the people working with him also understand it. Parents and teachers must know the aspects of his behavior that can be reversed through improvement in control—such aspects as hyperemotionality, inattention, and hyperactivity. Control is achieved by making the child aware of the unpleasant consequences of his behavior. If the behavior is part of the syndrome it must be incorporated into the treatment and the child is helped to learn to force himself to exert cognitive control; if the behavior is a reaction to the syndrome it is blocked whenever it occurs and alternative behaviors are offered. The clinician has his greatest role to play in assuring that the adults surrounding the child know how to deal with him and help him (Warren, 1965). The child usually does not need **psychotherapy** unless his relationships with his peers have so deteriorated that he is completely unable to interact with them; in this case a type of therapy is required that will provide experimental interactions from which the child can learn.

Brain Damage and Neurological Defects

The Strauss Syndrome is only one aspect of the broad problem of brain damage. A second aspect includes children who are both brain-damaged and retarded. The direct relationship between brain damage and learning disability is not clear (Rennick, 1966). History gives many examples of people who evidently suffered from brain damage but who performed at the genius level, among them Steinmetz, Louis XI, Mozart, and Gibbon. Logic would seem to tell us, however, that if part of the brain is obviously injured and if the person is also retarded, the injury caused the retardation, and there do seem to be conditions where there is a close relationship between retardation and the diagnosis of brain agenesis, dysgenesis, or injury.

In fact, it is highly probable that all mentally retarded people have some sort of brain impairment. A specific diagnosis of a brain impairment that possibly leads to retardation should never be taken as evidence that the person cannot be helped. All of the mentally retarded can be helped in some degree, and appropriate use of rehabilitation, remedial intervention, or therapeutic intervention is always in order (Haring, 1959; Argy, 1968). ("Remedial" refers to re-education and correction of both behavior and physical function; "therapeutic" refers to modification of personality, emotional disturbance, and social maladjustment.)

A third aspect of brain damage is seen in a group who do not have the symptoms of the Strauss Syndrome, but who do have neurological defects that can be determined clinically (Reitan, 1966; Knights & Ogilvie, 1967; Knights & Watson, 1968), and who do show various difficulties in functioning. It is hard to generalize about the problems of this group, partly because of the widely different ages at which the children may be afflicted (Reed & Fitzhugh, 1966) and the widely different conditions that result. The child who presents a post-**encephalitic** type of brain damage, for example, has a much different problem than does one who has a **congenital** malformation. Most of the differences between children in this group center around the function of the **memory bank** (Pribram, 1969); the child who has received brain damage late in the developmental period usually still retains the **memory** "deposits" that occurred before the damage, but the child who is damaged earlier will often have no such memories to fall back on and will almost inevitably be retarded.

The temporal succession in which the memory patterns are laid down seems to provide a continuity that later holds the elements of recollection together (Penfield, 1952; McGaugh, 1966). Thus the older child is able to remember many of his pre-**traumatic** experiences and is generally aware of his pre-traumatic development. But it is possible that the brain damage he has received will not permit new experiences or environmental patterns to be correctly recorded in some areas of the brain; in such a case he will have memory at one level of performance and information reception at another level, and the conflict will impede his ability to make appropriate decisions. The situation is further acerbated in cases of trauma in younger children or of profound trauma in older ones; the individual is not quite sure what he remembers, either because he was too young to complete the original memory or because the severity of the trauma has damaged some of the brain areas involved with memory. The resulting confusion often leads to violent reactions to the mildest kinds of intrusion (Rapaport, 1959, p. 269). There is evidence that part of the difficulty comes because such a child's greatest lack of memory is for recent events; thus he has older memory experiences that he cannot use and more recent behavioral experiences that he cannot remember (Pribram & Tubbs, 1966).

This memory factor probably is the reason that after brain damage, older individuals typically recover spontaneously over a period of time; eventually their memory for previous performance gives them sufficient guidance that they can begin once again learning new adjustment strategems and can accommodate or compensate for the effects of the trauma (Mackey, 1968). Younger children have no such information feedback available within themselves and therefore have more difficulty in making their own adjustment, but on the other hand they probably are more trainable because all of the information that they receive is new, and thus there are no conflicts between incoming stimuli and old memories. If the damage occurred at a sufficiently early age, however—probably during the first twelve months—the child will almost certainly be retarded, because his learning was cut off during the crucial period for brain development. Such a child's behavior may in many respects be reversible by training, but he will be unable to develop normal intellectual functioning without outside help (Baumeister & Hawkins, 1967).

Thus far we have the basis for several possible groupings of children: those with congenital malformations, with or without the Strauss Syndrome; those with **perinatal** (damage which occurs during the birthing process) or **neonatal** (damage which occurs immediately after birth) traumas or diseases, again with a wide variety of symptoms; and those who were damaged at a more advanced age and who typically do manifest the Strauss Syndrome. The first group are apt to be mentally retarded at the milder levels; the second group may range from not retarded to profoundly retarded but probably will have severe neurological problems; the third group are most likely to have severe emotional problems and learning disabilities. All three major groups present forms of behavior that can be reversed, but the children's ability to assimilate learning of the academic type is limited. One often must consider the economic status of the child and his family before deciding whether it is better to spend training time on academic subjects which he may learn poorly or on prevocational training which may serve him better in the long run.

Genius

In addition to these three major groups there is a fourth one that is an exception to most of the generalities we have thus far expressed. In members of this group the damage seems to result in a higher level of mental activity. Often people in this group are afflicted with various levels of **hydrocephaly** but we have no clear evidence as to why damage caused by enlarging the internal ventricles of the brain sometimes produces geniuses. About all that we can say is that brain damage causes abnormal brain functioning, and that in this group it causes abnormally superior functioning.

Aside from this small group of geniuses, however, obvious brain damage that can be clearly defined will impair learning rather than enhance it. If despite his brain injury the child has been able to maintain normal mentation he will be highly aware of the effects of the injury; he will know when he is not learning and when his siblings or peers can do things he cannot. We may expect psychological reactions to this knowledge, reactions that at times reach psychotic proportions (Simon, 1966).

The clinician has a dual responsibility in his therapeutic approaches to brain damage. First he must provide active psychotherapy (see Leland & Smith, 1965, Chapter VII), and second he must develop ways of letting the handicap serve as part of the therapeutic procedure (Sternlicht, 1965). This second function is best carried out by helping the child understand the consequences of his actions and letting him test alternative actions so that he can gain more self-confidence.

Sensory Defects

This therapeutic approach is equally valid with children who have outright sensory defects of various kinds; the child who must adjust to the loss of sight, hearing, or other sensory reception must learn through trial-and-error experience how to respond in an appropriate manner. First the child must have whatever medical correction can be achieved through hearing aids, spectacles, or other prosthetic devices, but beyond that he must in effect learn how to learn despite the physical defect.

The relationship between these sensory defects and mental retardation is by no means fixed, and may even be coincidental (Bialer, 1969), but there is an increased rate of hearing loss among the retarded (Lloyd & Reid, 1967; Lloyd & Frisina, 1965) which may or may not be related to differences in measured intelligence (Luszki, 1965); often the retardation and the hearing loss seem to have the same etiological base, e.g., **prematurity** (Mykelbust, 1958). Similar data have been collected for those with loss of sight, and it can be concluded that the relationship between blindness and retardation is coincidental (Lowenfeld, 1963; Elonen, Polzien, & Zwarensteyn, 1967).

Technically, many of the things we are describing may not be dysfunctions. If we are dealing with optical defects, for example, either in the eye or in the optic nerve, then the brain is not directly involved. We must assume, however, that anything that interferes with the reception of an appropriate signal is a brain dysfunction, because it interferes with the ability of the brain to function as it normally would. Sensory defects do interfere with learning and cognitive development, and as a result the brain cannot respond in a learning situation as it should. The connection between seeing and reading is the clearest, but the entire personal relationship of the child to his home, his peers, and his school depends heavily on his ability to sense them. Thus **sensory impairments** for practical purposes must be considered brain malfunctions.

When a child first puts on his glasses and says, "Gee, I can see the leaves on the trees," it is evident that previously he could not see them, or any of the other highly differentiated things which his peers could see. If he could not see them he could not react to them in the same way that a classmate reacted; although neither child would fully understand why, there would be feelings by one or both of them that somebody was wrong or irrational, and as the result of continued experiences of this sort the afflicted child would gradually become more confused and angry and less responsive to his peers.

The psychologist cannot be preoccupied specifically with the seeing or hearing problem itself, but there will be a great need for counseling associated with it; he must help the child accommodate to the glasses or the hearing aid and also help him deal with his angry feeling that he is not a part of what is going on around him. The basic need is to see that the child adapts to the difficulties that he faces. Often a child who has a partial disability will be at a greater disadvantage than the one who is totally disabled. If, as an example, he hears only part of what is going forward, he will fill in the missing parts by his imagination and often will develop an almost paranoid reaction to his peers because he supposes that the things he does not hear are somehow aimed at him. If the part that he misses really happens to involve him and he later realizes this, he may also feel that he is being left out on purpose. Thus children with partial hearing impairment are often marked by flashes of high anger.

The parent of a child with a disability of this sort must be constantly aware of what the child is missing—what he is not seeing or not hearing or not feeling—and must try to fill in the gaps with additional explanations. If the child feels totally informed about what is going on around him and what his role is expected to be, he will be much less inclined to suppose that things are being kept from him and thus less apt to respond with outbursts of bad temper. Should it develop that the child's condition can be helped by eyeglasses or a hearing device, he may upon first being given the aid become so confused by all of the additional stimuli which he suddenly receives, that his immediate reaction is again an outburst of anger. This response usually is temporary, but it demonstrates how much has been lacking in his environment up to that point and how much his parents, teachers, and clinicians must help him to understand even under those circumstances, so that he can complete the information that he was previously unable to gather during his whole lifetime.

When a child has a new prosthetic device of this sort, a major goal of the adults who work with him must be to see that the new sensory experiences he is receiving fill the gaps in his learning. Not only must they find ways to use his handicap as an aid to learning—a process we have already discussed in other contexts—but also to help both the child and the people around him to understand that even though he has the new device his background of experience is grossly different from that of his peers and thus he remains handicapped even though he has made an adjustment to the prosthesis. If those around him realize this fact, they can help to reduce the differences between his experience and others through continued explanation and help; thus they will bring him closer to normal interaction with his peers.

If a child has a sensory defect that cannot be aided by prosthetic devices, there is an additional adjustment problem. People who work with the blind emphasize such important matters as teaching them to read Braille or to walk freely; people who work with the deaf emphasize communication and other skills (Vernon & Brown, 1964) that let them function more normally. Such training is essential if the handicapped person is to become a functioning citizen. But there is another aspect of adjustment processes that more properly concerns us here; that is the control of the mannerisms and postures that children with sensory defects often unwittingly develop because they are not fully aware of their environment.

Blind children tend to develop mannerisms a great deal more than do seeing children. These **tics,** grimaces, and body postures that emerge as part of their general adjustment to growing up are known as **superstitious behavior,** because the behavior develops when the children make such motions and discover some new information or fail to make such motions and get hurt; in either event they then adopt the behavior as a desirable thing to do constantly even though in fact it is normally useless and undesirable. Closely allied are mannerisms—such as walking with a shuffle or general poor posture—which are adopted simply because they are convenient and the children have no models or guides that would lead them to do anything different.

Deaf children develop similar mannerisms related to their handicap because many normal responses are based on sound cues; thus they become socially visible because of their failure to respond in numerous situations, e.g., a failure to laugh. Other sensory defects also produce a variety of peculiarities that make the afflicted child visible as a handicapped person. All such handicapped children will be under much less pressure if they are taught to function as though they do not have the defect. Efforts should be made to teach them to assume more normal postures and be more concerned with the way they look to other people. This training is particularly difficult with blind children who not only cannot see how other people look and act, and thus cannot copy normal behavior, but who also tend to feel that because they themselves cannot see they are invisible to others.

Intervention must center around getting the child to understand how he looks to other people. This is done through his intact senses. With the blind, the sense of touch is usually most effective. A blind child must be given the opportunity to feel a smile, to feel good posture, to feel things that make sounds, and so on. He must learn through the feeling of laughter, for example, that certain things he does create unfortunate reactions. The therapist will overemphasize the reactions and should learn to respond in the manner of an actor in the old silent movies. Such exaggerated reactions are even more important in training the deaf child, who can begin to learn about emotional expression by seeing the difference between happiness and sadness and associating it with laughter or crying, even though he cannot hear them. In this way he also will begin to learn that when certain actions occur there is a special sentiment being reflected and that he will be more generally accepted if he can be a part of that sentiment instead of holding himself aloof from it.

Conversely, a child can be taught the real meaning of unresponsiveness. Here again the therapist must exaggerate; he must show total unresponsiveness beyond what the child has learned to expect. As the result of such teaching, children with sensory defects will begin to learn how normal people react to environmental stimuli and will be able to add those forms of behavior to their own repertoires. Then, building on those forms, they will much more readily utilize the special training they receive in necessary skills.

Convulsive Disorders

In addition to children who have sensory defects we must consider those who have **convulsive disorders.**[1] Once again, it is not the medical aspects of this type of brain dysfunction that should primarily concern the psychologist, but rather its relationship to learning. Any convulsion tends to cause brain damage in the sense of disrupting the brain functions and disorganizing brain cells (Pond, 1961), and thus produces an abnormal relationship between the individual and his environment. If the convulsions are strong enough and frequent enough, the individual's contact with his environment will be correspondingly strained; if they are even stronger and more frequent, his contact with his environment may be permanently severed. There is a

[1]There is an extensive literature on epilepsy and other convulsive disorders. The reader who desires a more thorough discussion should first see the two-volume set on *Epilepsy and Related Disorders* by Lennox (1960).

clear-cut relationship between the strength and incidence of convulsions and the learning difficulties of the child.

Convulsive disorders have a great influence on the personality of the affected person (Tizard, 1962). Whether he has the major convulsions of the pattern known as *grand mal* or the mild, barely discernible ones called *petit mal,* he normally will be aware of his situation, will see the effects that his seizures have upon others around him, will suffer from amnesia, and will be confused and frightened. Such a child loses motivation for learning. He is fatigued because of the physical effects of his attacks; he may be ashamed, particularly if he has wet himself or otherwise soiled his clothing during the convulsion (Hinton & Knights, 1966); and he will realize that his peers are frightened of him and that society in general either fears or pities him. As he grows older, unless the seizures are brought under control medically, the pity will give way to disgust and other people will avoid him or want to put him in an institution.[2]

Thus the first problem is that of seizure control. Without it, the victim not only forgets, as a result of his amnesia, the things that he has learned, but he is constantly faced with a painful, frightening, and unpredictable threat. He does not know when an attack is coming and he is unable to predict the consequences; he risks loss of bladder control, bowel control, or other bodily control. Further, there may be real physical injury if he hits his head or bites his tongue during a seizure. Such a child typically wakes up each morning wondering if today is the day that it is going to happen and goes to bed each night with some feeling or relief that it did not happen, but with the added threat that since it did not happen today it is more likely to happen tomorrow. He can scarcely be receptive to normal learning experiences, and the anger that characterizes children with various sensory defects is apt here to become a bitter hatred of a society that he feels is constantly saying, "There's that peculiar kid who has those crazy fits."

[2]One of the outstanding early physicians do describe epilepsy in modern terms was the Spaniard de Villanova (1240-1313). It is probable that epileptics were among the patients of the finer Spanish asylums such as the one at Valencia "known throughout Europe for its advanced administration and clinical facilities." (Alexander & Selesnick, 1966).

The child who suffers from *petit mal* may not be able to make the people around him understand that he "blacks out" temporarily. Then they will continue to make demands on him even though he cannot respond. His teacher may accuse him of not paying attention and his parents may adopt a "listen to me while I'm talking to you" attitude; he then will find that he constantly must defend himself because of behavior over which he has no control.

Today there is medical treatment available that will enable most epileptic children to make relatively good social adjustments. Even in past historical periods we find that Julius Caesar was epileptic[3] and that Napoleon had *petit mal;* if their afflictions did not impede their social progress there surely is little reason that most present-day epileptics cannot succeed.

Once the child receives proper medical attention, the psychologist faces the task of helping him adjust to his situation. The clinician will realize that the child feels he has been highly maligned and highly misused socially—sometimes with reason. He will explain that now he can lead a relatively normal, socially contributing life without being constantly in fear. Often medication for *grand mal* produces *petit mal* withdrawals; the child must be helped to recognize the minute symptoms that may signal him when such an attack is coming. The psychologist must also explain to parents and teachers not only the medical phenomena but also the psychosocial ones—for example, the child's feelings toward society—that are involved.

Cue Interpretation

All of the dysfunctions and associated learning handicaps that we have been discussing in this chapter have one primary point in common: they are related to social cue interpretation (Edmonson et al., 1967). There may be improper interpretation, improper cue priorities, or difficulty in attending to the proper cues. In other situations social

[3]Epilepsy may have been more common in the ancient world than we realize. The Greeks before Hippocrates (460-477 B.C.) described it as the "sacred malady" (Alexander & Selesnick, 1966).

interactions or organic problems interfere with the use of cues even though they are properly recognized. Sometimes the only identifiable symptoms are related to errors in cue interpretation and these errors are thus the factors first noted by teachers and parents.

The problem of cue identification and interpretation has led to a whole lore of psychological organicity and testing of brain damage. Determination of whether or not a child has brain damage is often left to the results of a psychological test, and numerous such tests have been developed. Failure to perform acceptably on the test supposedly marks the child as having some form of **central nervous system** disorder or organic disturbance. But much of the so-called organic testing in psychological laboratories or school classrooms actually merely test whether or not the child responds to the same cues in the same ways as the average child. Failure to respond appropriately to cues in drawing or manipulative tasks (Machover, 1949) is presumed to have an organic basis, while failure to respond to cues in **projective** tasks—such as the Rorschach test (Piotrowski, 1950) in which the child is asked to interpret **abstract** figures—is presumed to indicate emotional disturbance. But it has been hard to evolve research to establish the validity of these instruments. Certain gross responses may well indicate certain difficulties: a child who perseverates constantly on a projective test behaves in a manner suspiciously like that caused by a brain lesion, and one who gives clear evidence of impotency—as opposed to simply **negative** reaction—quite possibly suffers from a central nervous disturbance. But beyond that the diagnostic value of the tests is questionable.

One difficulty with such tests lies in deciding whether the child obtained no cues from the given data or whether he obtained miscues. A child who focuses on the wrong aspect of the problem may present a very good cue response to that wrong aspect. If he is asked to reproduce certain geometric figures but is unskilled at drawing, he may concentrate so hard on the drawing task that he ignores the differences between a diamond and a square. If he is asked to tell what is similar between two generally dissimilar objects and he lacks personal experience with one of the objects, he may concentrate on defining the strange object rather than meeting the requirements of the test as specified by the examiner. He may then try to hide or compensate for the misunderstanding and produce a wildly different response which is nonetheless highly creative and intelligent.

The situation is even more difficult when projective tests are used, because many of the responses that supposedly measure organicity can also be efforts to **compensate.** Undue use of time or constant repetition on the test can indeed be caused by organic factors, but they also can result when a child who is not quite sure how to respond is trying to "buy time," perhaps because he has the right answer but for some reason thinks it is not permissible. Efforts to compensate for misreading or not understanding cues lead to false diagnoses which cannot be verified biomedically in any way. A child may even make widely different scores on tests in the same battery. The examiner then must attempt to get into the child's frame of reference and see if he can determine why the scores were so different.

Each of these test results has its own kind of validity (Warren, 1968). As a result, the diagnosis is based more on the examiner's ability to interpret cues than on the child's, and diagnoses are based more on examiner differences than actual test performance (Achenbach & Zigler, 1968; Sanders, Zigler, & Butterfield, 1968). Further, diagnoses are often made on one or two responses to a test and we may find a psychologist making an important diagnosis such as "mental retardation due to some form of cerebral defect or malformation causing brain-damaged behavior" on the basis of relatively few test responses. In fact, with young children such diagnoses have even been made on the basis of zero responses, "corrected" statistically to make them scoreable (Wechsler, 1949).

Cues may be misread because of central nervous system disorders, or as we have seen they may be misread because of socio-cultural differences. They may also be misread because of social inference errors. The latter are caused by a child's inability to understand clearly the "social price of admission" or social rules in school, at home, or in the community (Edmonson, Leland, & Leach, 1968). In school, for example, he is supposed to talk only when the teacher gives permission; he is not supposed to throw things. If he does not understand these rules and goes his own way in the classroom, he is going to be in very great difficulty, which can be corrected only through counseling or re-education (Edmonson, Leach, & Leland, 1969).

Therefore instead of making diagnoses of organic disorders on the basis of missed cues in psychological tests, we are on much firmer ground if we say that misreading of test cues leads to abnormal responses, and that probably a child who consistently responds abnormally in test situations will also respond abnormally at home or in the school. Although the tests may not be valid for differential diagnosis, they probably are valid indicators of behavioral differences. The abnormal pattern needs no label of organicity or emotional disturbance, and the child probably will receive more effective psychological help if we simply state that his pattern differs from the norm and that this fact disrupts his relationship with his environment.

Where there is a clear-cut medical diagnosis, however, such as in the case of epilepsy, the child certainly must also receive the appropriate medical treatment, and the psychologist should make his approach to the child with the medical background in mind.

In Sum . . .

In this chapter we have considered relationships between organic defect or brain damage, various types of sensory and functional disabilities, and learning problems. The major point that these factors have in common seems to be an inability of the patient to recognize and interpret environmental cues. We have also in this chapter tried to lay to rest some of the older theories regarding brain injury and differential diagnosis—theories which do not contribute to effective help for the patient. At the same time we have made suggestions for professional intervention whenever possible.

7

Mental Retardation: A Paradigm

In the previous chapters we discussed forms of behavior that often are described as retarded but should not necessarily be so considered. Some functions and some behaviors, however, must definitely be considered as retarded. We do not want to become overly involved with differential diagnosis (Bialer, 1969), but in order to deal intelligently with mental retardation, something of a diagnostic approach is necessary.

Diagnosis needs to move away from the traditional intelligence test emphasis toward structured observations of behavior, tests of specific forms of behavior, and measures of specific learning processes. A diagnostic pattern would be one that assesses through (1) structured observations and tests, (2) the previous history of the child, (3) field observations of his present level of functioning, (4) the behavior generally expected of children of similar age, social origin, geographical area, etc., and (5) the anticipated developmental tasks for which the child must be prepared.

The aspect of diagnosis that involves the field observation of present functioning is the one with which we will be mainly concerned in this chapter. It deals with those features of present functioning which a professional observer would note from his knowledge of the broad ranges of behavioral and physical elements. As mental retardation can be said to exist only if there is demonstrable effect on the behavior of the child, field observation is an important early step toward diagnosis. The diagnosis emerges from the interaction of the observed elements with the other aspects of the diagnostic pattern, rather than from any specific single element.

In this chapter we will discuss both causes and observable aspects of functioning in the hope that a paradigm will become evident—an overall picture of mental retardation that will provide a better definition than can be given in a few words.

Our discussion so far of the various types of **developmental disabilities** has emphasized that mental retardation is not the appropriate term to use in relation to environmental deprivation or to children who have narrow learning disabilities but who may, for example, demonstrate extracurricular creative abilities and talents *(New York Review,* 1967*)*. Today a large number of children are designated as mentally retarded when there is no real need to label them in that way. Much as we dislike labels, however, they do have some utility. Different treatment procedures, different specific correction modes, and different modification elements require knowledge of the behaviors, conditions, or etiologies that we are trying to modify or correct. There is also a "bookkeeping" need for this information; in planning for treatment centers, schools, and programs we need statistics based on a firm definition, so that funds can be set aside for the needs of these particular children.

But in reference to any specific child, one must ask whether that child's needs require the program that accompanies the label. If he will benefit from the program, the child will find the label valuable. If his needs are not served by the program, the label is of no use to him. In our society, it is socially detrimental for him to carry a label that does not refer to a treatment or training need; the label "mental retardation" is not in itself bad, immoral, or destructive, but when promiscuously used with children who gain no benefit from it, it becomes all of these things.

AAMD Definition

The American Association on Mental Deficiency first introduced its definition for mental retardation in 1961.[1] Under the definition, the elements of subaverage general intellectual functioning, origin of the problem during the developmental period, and impairment in adaptive behavior are required before mental retardation can be considered to be present. If any one of these elements is missing the child should not be given the label even though he may have certain functional and learning deficiencies and may even benefit from the same type of program as that planned for the retarded. And even though all of the elements are present, the child still is not necessarily mentally retarded though he would certainly resemble very strongly those who are retarded. In other words, the definition is not diagnostic in itself, but it states the elements that are required to make a diagnosis in conjunction with other factors—such factors as the etiology of the problem, behavioral determinations such as measured intelligence and adaptive behavior, and associated environmental and social factors. The basic definition is merely a guide.

The AAMD (1973) set ten categories for a medical etiology of mental retardation. These categories try to relate physiological aspects of a person to his basic condition. A different approach is taken by the American Psychiatric Association (APA) in its *Diagnostic and Statistical Manual* (1968) which sets up essentially the same categories without attempting to assign etiological bases. In working with retarded individuals it has become clear that what formerly were called "knowable causes" of retardation are more accurately described as conditions associated with it. There need not be a direct relationship, even though most people who have certain biomedical conditions are mentally retarded. There is evidence that gross brain damage causes

[1]In 1973 the AAMD modified the wording of this definition to eliminate the "borderline" label but did not otherwise change the levels. The new definition reads: "Mental Retardation refers to significantly subaverage general intellectual functioning existing concurrently with deficits in adaptive behavior, and manifested during the developmental period." (Grossman, 1973)

certain types of behavior and that such factors as **chromosomal** structure may also influence behavior (Kaplan, 1969; Mauer, 1965), so that sometimes we can assign causes; this is true, however, only in a very small percentage of the people concerned. It is probable that every retarded person has some physiological or neurological error, but every individual who has those same errors is not necessarily retarded.[2]

These detailed classifications set up by the professional groups are valuable for the biomedical study of retardation, but they have less value for a social and psychological approach. For example, the largest group of mentally retarded persons is a sub-division under the major heading of "Environmental Influences"; a group described as "other." There is no known biomedical cause here, but these people function and give test results at a retarded level. In the past **"cultural-familial"** was used and this implied that there was a genetic tie, but this has not been demonstrated. What has been demonstrated is that most of those in this category come from areas of severe deprivation, malnutrition, improper disease control, and poor environmental support (Kugel & Parsons, 1967). They have in common a series of

[2]The AAMD classification system established the following ten etiological classifications:

(1) Infections and Intoxication.
(2) Trauma or Physical Agent.
(3) Metabolism or Nutrition.
(4) Gross Brain Disease (Post-Natal).
(5) Prenatal Influence.
(6) Chromosomal Abnormality.
(7) Gestational Disorders.
(8) Following Psychiatric Disorders.
(9) Environmental Influences.
(10) Other Conditions.

Each classification may be linked with any of the following supplementary conditions:

(1) Genetic Component.
(2) Secondary Cranial Anomaly.
(3) Impairment of Special Senses.
(4) Disorders of Perception and Expression.
(5) Convulsive Disorder.
(6) Psychiatric Impairment.
(7) Motor Dysfunction.

And in addition will have a behavioral classification based on measured intelligence (IQ) and adaptive behavior (Grossman, 1973).

behavioral and learning deficits growing out of their relationship to their environment; in general, they are the individuals who have not been able to cope appropriately, even within their own subgroup or among their own peers (Heber, 1961; Leland, Nihira, Foster, Shellhaas, & Kagin, 1968).

Environmental Influences

These youngsters, living in a low socioeconomic situation or in a minority culture stand out as deficient, even though the measured intellectual functioning of their whole community, as defined by criteria of the majority culture, is not high. Their behavioral responses to specific situations cause them to be rejected and called "stupid" by other children around them. Their behaviors are not as visible as those of emotionally disturbed children (they often tend to be more dull than violent), but they are not accepted by the gang, or at best are permitted to follow along or act as messenger boys because the gang does not know what else to do with them.

They are children who are judged retarded by their **peers.** This is not a matter of measurement, but rather of certain forms of behavior that clearly identify the child as being different. These forms usually are more related to social and personal maladaptation (Nihira, 1969a; 1969b) than to academic or skill functioning. A child who cannot hit a can with a rock may still be accepted by his peers, but if he shoves them while they are throwing their own rocks or if he arbitrarily knocks the can away with a stick, they will attack him. If he continually behaves in this way and—as is usually the case—if he also shows that he cannot fight in the accepted mode of the gang, he will be ostracized. Such a child is typically found to be mentally retarded (though he may also be emotionally disturbed).

Youngsters who suffer from a socially derived retardation have a different problem than other retarded persons. Some writers (Milgram, 1969; Zigler, 1967, 1969; Winick, 1970) even try to separate the two categories completely, implying that the children who fall under the "cultural-familial" pattern are anatomically and physically sound, as opposed to those who are retarded because of evident biomedical factors. This implication does not hold up under examination, however; people may well have subtle damage that is not obvious and give no outward sign of it except their retarded behavior. Many individuals who would be classified as cultural-familial because they have no clear-cut medical etiology are severely retarded[3] while others who are clearly impaired physically may be capable and intelligent—for example, Primo Carnera, Michael Dunn, or Steinmetz. But what *can* be said is that the socially-derived retarded, far more than any of the other categories, are produced through an interaction between social factors, disease factors, and malnutrition (Scrimshaw & Gordon, 1968; Eichenwald & Fry, 1969).

Malnutrition seems to play the greatest role with this group, although not necessarily malnutrition of the person himself. The malnutrition of his mother (Winick, 1970) and of her parents can cause a general inability to cope and lead to a form of retardation which has no specific etiology. The behaviors of this group of children tend to be reversible (Skodak, 1968), and this fact has raised the question as to whether they really should be described as retarded. But we must say that a person who functions at a retarded level at any given time is retarded at that time; if his behavior is reversed so that later he no longer functions in a retarded way, the fact cannot alter the initial behavior. Otherwise we are faced with the misleading and even damaging concept of pseudo-retardation, which we discussed earlier (Chapter 3). The preoccupation with labeling the retarded person leads to much greater confusion than simply accepting the behavior as below that which society can tolerate. Having accepted that, one can go immediately into the rehabilitation, treatment, or behavior modification procedures that are required to bring his behavior up to a tolerable level (Royal Commission, 1957).

[3]Historically those with the most profound biomedical involvement did not live, so that those who survived were more mildly afflicted; but as we think of their behaviors they represent varying degrees of severity and some probably survived because of the accident of high birth, e.g., Peter III of Russia, Nero of Rome. Thus even this general kind of delineation in terms of functional behavior cannot be used.

Field observation of "environmental" retardation is particularly necessary in arriving at a diagnosis. Diagnosing it is not a question of measurement; we have seen (Chapter 3) that despite current special education labeling practices, measurement of IQ among cultural minorities such as blacks or Mexican-Americans can range from pointless to misleading.[4] The only appropriate indication of this kind of retardation is the inability of a child to keep pace with his peers from a similar cultural background.

Prenatal Influence

Another large group of retarded have an etiology related to **intrauterine** trauma during the period of gestation. Some workers in the field consider this the dominant cause of retardation (Pevzner, 1959; Crome & Stern, 1967). They believe that they can trace conditions of physiological and anatomical malformation to various insults during the first or second trimester of development (see the early research of Ingalls, Curley, & Prindle, 1952). The basic proposition is that the conception was normal but that something happened to the mother immediately after conception or during the gestation period. Such an insult may cause chromosomal irregularities which may have either a genetic basis related to the concept of mutations (Kaplan, 1969), or, as in **Down's Syndrome,** some other exogeneous factor (Carter, Hamerton, Polani, Gunlap, & Weller, 1960; Carter & Evans, 1961; Ellis & Delhanty, 1960; Jacobs, Baikie, Court-Brown, & Strong, 1959; Coleman & Stoller, 1962; Forsfman & Lehmann, 1962). The individuals who suffer from intrauterine damage vary considerably in intelligence, ranging from those who are profoundly retarded and who typically do not survive past the fourth or fifth year to those who have relatively mild retardation but obvious malformation.

[4]Failure to understand this phenomenon has led a whole group of scholars to falsely assume a relationship between IQ, learning potential, and genetic endowment (e.g., Jensen, 1969).

Prenatal Care and Prematurity

Prematurity, one of the single most important factors in retardation, is closely associated with a third major group. It has been estimated that at least 50 percent of all premature children are neurologically damaged in some way (President's Panel, 1962). In this context, prematurity refers to both the weight of the child at birth and the length of the gestation period; it means an under-developed baby, and the implications are that such a child is already impaired and has a diminished opportunity to develop properly (Knoblock, Pasamanick, Harper, & Rider, 1959). He is less able to cope with the natural demands of his environment, and if he survives it will be at a lower state of functioning (Moore, 1965). There is a close tie with the socioeconomic (Wortis & Freedman, 1965) and moral framework of the community, for there is a direct relationship between prematurity and **prenatal** care (President's Panel, 1962).

It hardly need be pointed out that those least able to get appropriate prenatal care are in low socioeconomic areas, but the problems caused by moral codes may be less evident. Here we deal mainly with the matter of illegitimacy; many young girls, particularly those of high school age, become pregnant but keep away from medical care because as minors they will be the subjects of special reports and investigation, and in some cases social ostracism. Usually such girls do not know an appropriate doctor and are afraid to seek help. Society takes the paradoxical approach of neither making abortions readily available to them nor of providing the means to protect the unborn infant. Usually these mothers receive no medical attention until the pregnancy is physically obvious, which is three or four months too late as far as the child is concerned. Sometimes also the young mother will still be too immature for motherhood, will not yet be hormonally complete, and thus will not be able to provide the child the necessary biological support during its prenatal development. Some young mothers also may attempt or submit to illegal and unsuccessful abortions, thus damaging their children. All of these factors contribute to the rate of prematurity.

The behavior both of those individuals resulting from intrauterine trauma and of those resulting from prematurity demonstrates a wide range of developmental lags and failures.

Infection and Toxic Agents

Another major group of etiologies is that caused by infection and toxic agents before and during birth. **Rubella** is a clear-cut example of infection that produces malformations and related retardation with an estimated defect rate of 90 percent (lin-Fu, 1968 ; Baylor Rubella Study Group, 1967; Cooper, 1966; Rubella, 1967). The effect of maternal intoxication, toxic states, drugs and narcotics as they relate to the birth processes, needs further examination (Klosovsky, 1968), as does the relationship of toxic states and hormone production (*Hormone & Behavior,* 1969). At present, however, all we really can say is that babies born under these conditions show many peculiar reactions at birth.

Mechanical Injuries

Yet another group of retarded are caused by mechanical injuries. Under this heading comes damage caused by attempted abortions, plus the whole range of possible **postnatal** injuries. Here much of the diagnosis is based on the case history. Mechanical injuries probably are the least common causes of retardation, but they are the ones most often cited; many mothers remember when their retarded children fell out of highchairs or received other bumps on their heads, and assume that these caused the condition. One reason for the frequency of this parental reaction may be that it helps to stem feelings of guilt that the parents did something to cause the retardation or that they provided genetic factors that led to the condition.

Among those suffering from mechanical injuries are the ones who come under the classification of "the **battered child** syndrome"—in other words, outright child abuse. These are cases of purposeful injury, where the baby has been unmercifully beaten and in the process has been damaged (Johnson & Morse, 1968; Elmer, 1967). Child abuse has been defined as "non-accidental, physical attack or physical injury, inflicted upon children by persons caring for them" (Helfer & Kempe, 1968). Such abuse often is not reported because of lack of specific evidence. Recently some states, notably Kansas, in cooperation with Brandeis University have set up legal procedures for the establishment of central registers for "abuse or suspected abuse" cases (Martin, 1968).

Generally head injuries creating **cerebral trauma** must be extremely severe to produce retardation, and the fact of damage is apparent either through coma or clearly visible with X-ray evidence of skull damage—or through a history of these symptoms. Such cases have a good record of a positive prognosis. However, the younger the child the more permanent will be the damage to areas of cognitive functioning.

Mal-presentation during birth, cord around the neck, forceps injuries, failure of the child to respond properly to oxygen after birth, **anoxia,** and similar causes all may produce some retardation. Forceps delivery probably is most often accused of birth injuries, but the accusation generally is not correct; deep forceps are only used if something else has already gone wrong and usually the other cause is the real one. There is also a rather low incidence of immediately postnatal problems such as **anoxemia** and suffocation. Babies born in a hospital with proper obstetrical attention have a better chance than those born at home or in understaffed clinics; the inability of a mother to have appropriate medical attention at the time of birth contributes greatly to the risk of damage.

Overview

This review of etiology and its observable results is not intended to be comprehensive, but rather to highlight the areas typically identified with mental retardation. The related social and environmental elements tie in very closely to the biomedical elements. There are a vast number of **developmental anomalies** defects that contribute to retarded mental functioning; these are acted upon by an equally vast number of environmental factors which may actually determine whether or not the infant grows up to be retarded. Most of the conditions that we have described are formed by the socioenvironmental forces that surround the family (1) at the time of conception, (2) during the first six months of gestation, and (3) during the perinatal and immediate postnatal periods. If those forces can be modified or changed, the incidence and prevalence of the conditions will be considerably lowered (New York State, 1955; Lemkau & Imre, 1969).

Once the retardation has been created, however, the person must have help. The most profoundly damaged individuals probably cannot be rehabilitated, but even they usually can be helped in some manner to modify their coping skills; and they are the ones from whom we gain knowledge of the condition and its possible prevention. If we are dealing with exogenous environmental influences, modifications of those influences and the possible resultant correction of deficiencies can occur if the modification is attempted at a sufficiently early age. Early intervention can make a very important difference in the final outcome even though it may not be able to bring the child to a normal level.[5] The child certainly can be brought to do more for himself with help than if he is left to his own devices or put into an institution where he might deteriorate (Wolfensberger, 1969). We must forget the mythology that the retarded who have certain clearly defined etiologies cannot be helped (Leland, 1969).

The behavioral classification of the AAMD is based on measured intelligence, as represented by the IQ, and on adaptive behavior (Leland, Nihira, Foster, & Shellhaas, 1968). At this point we will not go into a discussion as to whether intelligence follows a normal distribution; there is some evidence that it does not (Girardeau, 1969). We cannot in any event assume on a purely statistical basis that a certain portion of mankind is going to be mentally retarded.

[5]Recent research in malnutrition indicates that corrective intervention must occur before ten weeks of age or the total *number* of available brain cells will be permanently reduced. That failing, intervention must be made before three years of age or the *size* of the existing cells will be permanently reduced (Winick, 1970).

Subaverage intellectual functioning implies intellectual functioning below the norm of the group being measured. Thus if the group is relatively high even "significantly subaverage" will mean something entirely different than would be true in a lower group. There is little need to further belabor the fact that the IQ is a poor device for judging whether or not a child is retarded. The general aspect of measured intelligence more properly deals with the relationship of the child to socially defined learning tasks (Bortner & Birch, 1970).

According to the AAMD definition, the physical condition recognized as a possible cause of the retardation must occur during the developmental period. If the brain of an adult is damaged in an auto accident or similar occurrence, he may function for a time at a retarded level and may have a lowered IQ, but unless the damage is very profound he probably will not be considered mentally retarded. Impairment in infancy not only involves the impaired brain area, but also severely hinders the ability to gain and use skills which are usually acquired through contact and communication with the child's culture. Severely impaired adults who already have gained these skills may lose some of them because of an accident, but they seldom will lose enough to be considered mentally retarded (Halstead & Rennick, 1966).

The other aspect of the classification, adaptive behavior,[6] is the most important one. Practically speaking, we can see that this is true; a child who has low measured intelligence and specific malformations, but who adapts so sufficiently that he is not socially visible, is unlikely to be considered retarded by his cultural group. On the other hand, the one who is noisy, angry, and throws rocks probably will be institutionalized. The difference is purely in adaptive behavior. In fact, social maladaptation of this kind is a major cause of institutionalization (Shellhaas & Nihira, 1969; 1970).

[6]Adaptive behavior has been defined as "the manner in which the individual copes with the natural and social demands of his environment." It includes the elements of independent functioning, personal responsibility, and social responsibility (Heber, 1961; Grossman, 1973; Leland, et al., 1968).

Therefore a child who has developed appropriate coping skills and is functioning at an appropriate level of adaptive behavior is not retarded. This is true even though his social awareness, sensory-motor development, or rate of learning may be limited. Conversely, if his adaptive behavior is impaired he may well appear to be retarded even if the other aspects of his intelligence are at an acceptable level (Leland, 1973).

Thus the observable aspects of retarded functioning, which we have considered together with etiology in this chapter, are the most important ones in our initial approach to a diagnosis. Again we must emphasize that an effective diagnosis requires consideration of all the factors of the diagnostic pattern, even though society at times makes demands that may result in children being diagnosed as mentally retarded without all of the pieces being in place. Such demands may be caused by over-burdened welfare rolls or over-populated schools, but they should be resisted. Generally, mental retardation exists only if all of the factors indicate it and if there is a demonstrable effect on the behavior of the child.

8

Current Management Models

This chapter will describe the current methods of providing management services to the mentally retarded. When the mentally retarded person has sufficient **adjustment** difficulties within his community to require management services, the outstanding feature of the services delivered, as distinguished from services for almost any other clinical group, is that they most often start at the institution and work back into the community.

It is striking that *the* method always thought of first is the institution. Usually it will be a state hospital or school, although more affluent families may look toward a private institution. In either case the pattern is the same: the first answer automatically is to place a retarded child in the institution. Only as a second thought, perhaps because there is a waiting list for the hospital or school, do parents usually consider community services. Both parents and service agencies tend to look upon these services—day-care centers, **sheltered environments,** mental retardation or child-guidance clinics—as temporary. A third choice will be the family doctor, a preferred teacher, school psychologist, or a member of the family who may assume responsibility for delivering the services. Of all clinical groups, the mentally retarded are almost the only ones for whom the automatic first choice of society is the most extensive, most drastic, and most expensive way of providing services.

Residential Institutions

It becomes axiomatic that one of the major problems associated with present management services is the fact that the child is in an institution. The large general residential institutions typically consist of mentally retarded individuals of both sexes, with all five levels of measured intelligence. (Moving from least to most retarded, these are Borderline, Mild, Moderate, Severe, and Profound. At present they are based on IQ ranges.) There usually are some representatives of most of the ten major etiological categories (see footnote 2, Chapter 7). In addition there is a large variety of orthopedically handicapped, sensorially handicapped, epileptic, and psychiatrically impaired children and adults who have secondary and tertiary handicaps associated with mental retardation (that is, the **primary handicap** is the mental retardation; if, as an example, a patient also had epilepsy, that would be a **secondary handicap;** then if he had a skull anomaly, that would be a tertiary handicap—they are listed in order of most mentally handicapping to least). The largest group comes from that category known as cultural-familial, and the greatest number of these people have what are essentially behavioral disorders associated with learning deficiencies and cultural deprivation (Shellhaas & Nihira, 1969; 1970).

Such institutions often are very large, with populations ranging up to 6,000 (AAMD, 1968). Staffing is limited. There even seems to be an inverse ratio between the size of the staff and the number of the patients; institutions with 600 patients may have as many as six psychologists while institutions with 3,000 patients may also have six psychologists (Kugel & Wolfensberger, 1969). Yet one of the rationales for maintaining large residential institutions has been that certain kinds of major services would be available there that are not available in smaller organizations. The public gets an image of a vast hospital with modern, up-to-date equipment. This is not only untrue, but if it were true it would not be serving the majority of the patients, who do not require vast, modern hospital facilities. They are not ill, they are uneducated and maladapted.

Another contradiction is that the largest institutions usually have the largest waiting lists (Rudin, 1964). This is in part because those communities that insist on removing retarded children from society are also those who successfully resist their return. It also is because hospitals and state schools have so improved their medical practices that their death rates have greatly declined, and as the death rates declined the number of available spaces also declined. Virtually all of the large general state residential institutions today are warehouses for children, concerned with keeping their classifications straight, maintaining an adequate level of general health and a certain amount of clinical, educational, and medical services. Large private institutions are essentially the same, although they usually have a more comfortable ratio of staff to patients.

This is not to say that large general institutions fail to carry out any rehabilitation programs, but rather that their programs are much less effective than they could be under other circumstances. A patient in such an establishment can spend a full day without ever having to make a social decision. Although he probably will go through some programs of clinical and educational modification, these will not deal fully with his adaptive needs nor be able to teach appropriate coping skills, and if he is returned to his community he still is apt to be lonely, isolated, and highly visible.

The President's Committee on Mental Retardation has given a full overview of the current status of public institutions (Kugel & Wolfensberger, 1969). The point it underlines is that the current models are neither adequate to the needs of the retarded child, nor is the philosophy on which they were developed consistent with the needs of the nation to maintain the highest levels of humanity. These institutions cannot fit our current thinking in the area of rehabilitation, behavior modification, or clinical intervention (Wolfensberger, 1969). Both their physical plants and the theoretical bases for their existence are inappropriate to our current needs. This is true of all state general residential settings and is not intended just to emphasize those which are actually doing a very bad job. The report of the committee mentions institutions which are obviously mistreating their patients and which are typically thought of as "snake pits," so these types of settings do still exist; but if they were cleaned up and brought to the level of the better institutions as conceptualized in current philosophy, they would still not be solving the problem (Blatt, 1970).

Society's historical answer to the problems with retarded children has centered around grouping them into some sort of institutional setting. This goes back to the decision of the Council of Nicala in 325 A.D. (Payne, 1916), and in varying degrees these traditions seemed to have been with us ever since. Sometimes the greatest emphasis has been on care; sometimes it has been on medical treatment; sometimes it has been on specific etiologies. More often it has been based on other factors such as a supposed need to protect society, or a supposed need to protect the child regardless of the basis, or just pity for the child. But the whole history of care has centered around some sort of institutional consideration when dealing with the retarded or with retarded children (Kanner, 1967). Often the education or vocational training of the mentally retarded in these institutions has been quite adequate (Doll, 1967), but the failure to handle the need for socialization and "human" activities has made the institutions very degenerative and depersonalizing places even when they have had adequate or appropriate rehabilitation programs. It was this contradiction that led many professionals to begin looking at other aspects of training, particularly those relating to social competence (Doll [1953] presented the first form of the Vineland Social Maturity Scale in 1935).

The history is not entirely negative; that is, children who do not find within their own family the adequate level of help to deal with their problems certainly need some additional help from state services. Historically it has been generally true that this type of additional help could not be provided to the child directly in his own home. The major factors preventing it have been poverty, illiteracy, and lack of education, as well as the typical situation found in overcrowded slums and other disease-producing areas. So the concept of taking these children out of that environment and placing them into a more structured and supposedly more beneficial environment was not always entirely wrong. The evil comes from the nature of the environment into which the child is placed and the lack of continued public concern for him after his placement.

A typical community hospital, for example, is an institution, and people must go there from time to time to deal with specific needs. Such a hospital can also become a "snake pit" if public surveillance is not maintained, but the traditional relationship between the community and its medical facilities has been such that today an individual may safely enter most hospitals, receive appropriate treatment, and leave without incurring additional psychological or physical injury. The fact that the hospital is an institution does not make it an evil thing. The problem with our institutions for the retarded is that this concept of going in, receiving help, and *leaving,* has not yet become part of our thinking.

The difficulty arises as much from the nature of a general institution as it does from its size. There is a tendency in such an institution, whether large or small, to reduce all patients to the lowest common denominator (Dokecki, 1964). Regardless of the goodwill of the staff or the amount of equipment, the probability remains that the place will produce universal approaches to individual problems. The resulting depersonalization, the lack of appropriate interpersonal relationships, the lack of mobility, and the loss of access to general society, all contribute to a large degree of personal deterioration (Townsend, 1962).

This inevitable result of general institutionalization is made even worse by the usual attitudes about the mentally retarded. If the retarded person is considered an animal, that implies he will behave in a primitive, uncontrolled fashion (Vail, 1967). Institutions are typically designed to be indestructable, with unbreakable, shatter-proof wire-and-mesh glass, with reinforced partitions. The most heavy-duty furniture available is used. Walls and floors are made of materials that are hard to deface and easy to hose down.

Soundproofing is often installed to muffle noises, even in rehabilitation areas designed for patients who are well able to learn appropriate adaptive behavior.

Further, the retarded person is often considered potentially assaultive, destructive, and lacking in self-direction or constructive purpose. Thus his movements must be restricted, both to control him more easily and to protect him from the other "subhuman" individuals around him. As a result the institution has locked living units, doors that lock only from the outside, and fences or walls around the buildings or the entire installation. Because the patient is not thought capable of meaningful choices, he is permitted little control over his environment and even the light switches are made inaccessible to him. There is an implication that he is being "kept" rather than treated, and any interaction that he has with the staff is held at a minimum.

There is much more emphasis here on the use of drugs to control behavior than on the forces of human interaction. The general approach is that the individual cannot take care of his own needs in any way. This state of "subhumanity" is perceived to be essentially permanent and so the environment is designed to maintain a level of functioning that cannot provide opportunities for further growth and development. Once admitted, the child is expected to remain under this care for the rest of his life (Vail, 1967).

These conditions are still quite typical today. Some institutions have changed their attitudes and have attempted to provide more normal living opportunities, but they are still general institutions and the need for an organized, unified structure still makes it impossible for a patient to maintain appropriate control over his own daily activities. Any attempt to make a personal decision such as is typical of normal childhood will probably cause the individual to be punished because he is deviating from administrative routine. This not only blocks maturity but often produces extreme emotional upsets as well, and they add to the person's deterioration (Duche & Lortholary, 1968).

Regional Facilities

One plan to mitigate institutional conditions is to set up regional institutions; the thought is that if there are 2,000 patients who need to be in an institution, you can place them in one large establishment or in five smaller ones with 400 patients each. Certainly there are some advantages to the smaller institutions; there can be increased interactions between the patients in them and sometimes it is easier to get professional staff members who thus can remain in their home areas. The disadvantages are greater than the advantages, however. First, the theory of the zone plan is faulty. The idea that a child with Down's Syndrome (a chromosomal disorder associated with physical stigmata and moderate to severe retardation) from one section of a state has more in common with a cultural-familial child from that section than he has with a child with Down's Syndrome from a different part of the state is ridiculous. It would seem to be much more effective to group all Down's children for a short period of intensive study and then return them home or to a community residential equivalent. (And we might add as an aside, the cultural-familial child should not have been placed in an institution in the first place.)

Zone plans group all children regardless of need on the basis of place origin. This does create a convenience by maintaining child-parent interaction, but this same convenience can be better maintained by expanding local facilities and family support.

The answer to bigness is not necessarily littleness. In a zonal institution most of the evils of the large, general, residential facility have been maintained, but on a smaller scale. Thus it remains a general institution and cannot give the specialized care that is needed for effective rehabilitation. Second, while such an establishment can attract indigenous staff members it should not be dependent only upon them; it needs a variety of staff with a variety of backgrounds; and as it usually is placed in a remote setting it will have difficulty in drawing good professional people to an area far from any intellectual stimulation.

Third, while it remains a general institution it probably becomes a poorer general institution than the large, centralized school or hospital; the large place can afford expensive, specialized equipment and the trained people to use it, e.g., EEG machines, but if the same expenditures are split into five parts, probably none of the five institutions can afford such facilities or staff. Certain types of programs and certain kinds of vitality which can be present in a specialized state institution are lost in a generalized zone setting. The problem centers not only on size, but also on the generalist nature of the institution; changing the first without dealing with the second may actually make matters worse.

As children grow up in an institution their behavior as young adults reflects their lack of contact with normal people during their developmental period. This is also noted from periods of early development; there is a decided difference between children raised in a regular home environment and those raised outside such a home, with the lack of family care that this implies (Provence & Lipton,1962). If such patients are returned to a more typical family environment, some of the loss will be regained but usually they still will show noticeable sociopsychological difficulties. The older the child and the longer he remains away from a normal community, the greater the problem.

This overall pattern of dehumanization and isolation from normal peers which we have been describing establishes for the individual a new way of life. He adopts living modes and coping strategies that are appropriate to the institution and appropriate to his self-preservation and personal maintenance within the demands of that setting. This very adjustment becomes one of the major difficulties, because even though he may successfully meet the standards of rehabilitation within the institution (having completed their educational or vocational program), he still is not a good discharge candidate—these other factors have made him an alien outside the institution. Regardless of how much institutional training a person may have, the normal demands of everyday living in the outside community negate his ability to utilize that training if he has not had any experience with the demands of that community. Thus, the real evils of the general institution do not rest in its size and perhaps, in fact, not even in the isolation but rather in the factors that (1) it is general, thus reducing all patients to the same need standards and (2) that it retains the individual during the essential developmental period, making any adaptation to another setting very difficult.

Thus the argument as to whether or not one should maintain a medically oriented "hospital" or an educationally oriented "school or training center" (Ostrom, Rosenblood & Hubbard, 1971), is relatively useless and irrelevant. The expressed value of the hospital approach was that individuals were supposed to receive treatment and then leave. This is still a valid concept, but we know that in practice the majority of mentally retarded individuals do not need medical treatment and that the treatment they do receive does not provide them with the means of leaving, unless this treatment is on a short-term, specific basis for a particular ill.

The first and most important solution to the problem of institutionalization might be to bar the doors to a great percentage of children.[1] It makes little difference whether the institution is called hospital or school, whether it is supposedly medically oriented or educationally oriented; in either case the child is trained to live in an institutional setting, and thus learns many of the very things that we do not want him to learn. Ideally, all present institutions should be barred to further admissions until broader, more effective long-range programs can be worked out. Of course, this will only take place when community facilities and programs are developed.

Community Agencies

Community service agencies comprise a variety of individual services and may encompass more than one local community (PL-89-10; PL 88-164; PL 88-156; PL 89-333; PL 91-517), though also in large metropolitan areas there may be more than one service agency. The tendency, however, is to develop community clinics and **comprehensive centers** that cover a wide area; one comprehensive clinic in Kansas includes more than twenty counties and serves a catchment area greater than four New England states. Such community services still consider the mentally retarded children to be temporary patients. Usually they accept such children only for the testing and diagnosis required for admission to an institution; should the institutional waiting list be a long one, the parent may then reapply for help

[1]It is interesting to note that Howe made a similar suggestion in 1866, but unfortunately his warning was ignored (Wolfensberger, 1969, p. 140).

during the waiting period. Some community service areas have begun to equip themselves to meet this need with day-care centers, **sheltered workshops,** and sheltered environmental areas, and there are even some comprehensive mental retardation clinics, designed, however, to deal with immediate aspects of the problem on a short-range basis.

The day-care centers are one of the greatest areas of potential help, but at present they are one of the greatest areas of difficulty. They have two major problems, a lack of programming and a lack of availability. Typically, a day-care center is operated by a local parents' group with only limited professional support. It performs a baby-sitting function with some minor educational objectives. The baby-sitting part is valuable—it enables the child to interact socially with other children at his level, and it gives his mother a much-needed respite to do other things besides caring for him—but the service would be much more valuable if it also provided better programs for the child.

These centers do, however, enable more children to remain at home rather than going into institutions. Parents are much more willing for a retarded child to be at home if they can have some relief from the burden of constantly taking care of him. Those retarded children who come from fairly comfortable environments make good use of the parent-operated day-care centers, but they account for only ten percent of the total need. The large mass of mentally retarded youngsters come from low socioeconomic areas, have major learning difficulties, and do not fit into this type of day-care center; their needs are different and they do not have the money. With the exception of a program currently found in the state of Michigan,[2] the public has not supported the growth of **child-development centers,** which are what the economically deprived children actually need.

The various attempts at sheltered environments face similar problems. Prevocational training is maintained in many large school systems for the educable child (usually defined as having an IQ over 50 and under 80), who quite

[2]Information about this program may be had from the Day Care Center Program, State Department of Mental Health, Lansing, Michigan.

often does not need it because he can be taught to fit the work patterns of the community; but such training is almost totally nonexistent for the trainable child (usually defined as having an IQ over 30 and under 50). In dealing with the mentally retarded, training must start early and continue over a long period with much repetition and duplication; ideally it should start when a child is ready for kindergarten, or even before then. Further, children from a low socioeconomic level need a totally sheltered environment rather than just a sheltered work environment; they need such help as an improved nutritional level and disease protection.

The usual community response, however, is that if a child needs this additional protection he should be put in an institution—a fantastically expensive approach monetarily and a fantastically wasteful one in terms of human lives. The need for sheltered community environments which provide on the one hand educational and clinical care and on the other nutritional and preventive medical care is great, but the facilities are totally lacking.

That very rare thing, a comprehensive community clinic for the mentally retarded, can be found in a few places. Such clinics are hampered by the superstition that services for the mentally retarded must be kept separate from those for the emotionally disturbed or the other categories who need help. However, there is no reason whatever that facilities for retarded children cannot go under the same roof as facilities for emotionally disturbed children. In fact, even on the professional level, the kinds of intervention required depend not on the diagnostic classification of the child, but on his specific forms of behavior (Leland, 1968).

Although procedures used with the mentally retarded may differ from those used with the emotionally disturbed because of behavioral distinctions, the same psychologist can apply both. In medical intervention, the surgical procedure for an appendix operation differs from that for a gall bladder operation, but normally the same surgeon can do either one; only in very unusual cases would we call for an appendix specialist or a gall bladder specialist. Similarly, intervention to modify or train different behaviors can be done by the same psychologist, except again in the most specialized cases. And though it is inconceivable that anyone would build an appendix hospital and a gall bladder hospital side by side, that is just what we do when we build mental health or child guidance clinics on the one hand and mental retardation clinics on the other. Or more typically, we build only mental health clinics and they do not treat the retarded. The result of this separation policy has been to block the development of new services for retarded children instead of increasing them as the federal legislative provisions intended (PL 88-164).

Neighborhood Services

Because of federal legislation, the term "community services" has acquired the connotation of an organized and specialized function. Thus we need another term to distinguish a lower-level and less differentiated service, and the term **"neighborhood services"** has been adopted. This is not a semantic quibble but simply a different name that is needed for a different kind of service. Neighborhood services are the remaining services within the locality that carry on the regular day-to-day health, education, and general welfare functions. The normal response of those services to the presence of a visibly retarded child is "we must do something about it." That is a good reaction, but local services frequently become confused over who can be helped, the professional people consulted may not be familiar with retardation, and the result usually is one of two extremes: either pressure builds to separate the child from society or the parents are assured that he probably will outgrow his condition. We have considered most of the arguments against separation, and we know that retardation left to its own devices is not outgrown. Putting off the parents' concern delays treatment. Often the parents let the matter drop; this tendency may help to account for the extremely low percentage of retarded persons reported at the preschool level (New York, 1955).

The most typical neighborhood contact is the private physician or public health nurse. Both are sincere, but both often lack specific experience with mental retardation. They particularly lack information about matters that are not reflected in clear-cut biomedical problems; these are such things as cognitive development and child development as it relates to learning. The problem increases as we move from rural to urban areas. In a rural area the doctor often has known the family through more than one generation and during a number of births, and therefore he has a basis of comparison and a greater likelihood of sensing that something is not quite right with a given baby. He then can search with the parents for the right procedures to follow. But in urban areas doctors see large numbers of children on routine visits and tend either to examine them physically for specific ills or to respond to the symptoms their parents describe. If the examination gives negative medical results, other possibilities frequently are not considered. A similar process occurs when school or community clinics give mass tests or inoculations. In either event the parents come away feeling that they have a healthy child, which they probably do, but with no information about possible learning disorders or retardation.

When the Child Enters School

Additional professional people become available when the child enters school; there are school psychologists, counselors, and special education teachers. Usually they become aware of a highly visible child rather quickly. By that time it may be five years too late for the child, but at least some consideration is then given to his learning processes. These professionals, however, usually are attuned to **educable mental retardation (EMR)** and should the child not fit this category the tendency is to exclude him from school. If the school system has **trainable mental retardation (TMR)** classes he may be included in one of them, but few systems offer them because they require special architectural provisions and other modifications of facilities as well as modifications of the special education curricula. School systems also have a variety of ways of defining the educable category, so that the EMR child in one school may not closely resemble his supposed counterpart in another school, thus adding to confusion.

Special education classes usually contain a mixed collection of children, often of types that should have quite different programs. Yet most of the largest group of retarded children, the cultural-familial classification, may not be found in special education classes; there are so many of them that whole schools tend to fall into this academically retarded category if they are in ghetto or poverty areas. In such schools, special education classes include only the most visible youngsters whom regular teachers cannot control, and will concentrate more on baby sitting than on special programs. The regular classrooms in these schools tend to become arenas of constant warfare between teachers who try to present material drawn from their cultural background and children who find the material completely out of the context of their world. Rarely do we find any special curricula designed to keep these disadvantaged students from becoming retarded. Thus many of these children come into school from a deprived economic background, they find school to be a source of conflict rather than learning, and there are no special plans to meet their needs; the result is academic retardation leading eventually to a learning turnoff and functional retarded behavior.

A final consideration is a child's family.[3] Although a family is not a service agency in the usual sense, it often provides the only services a child receives while he is still a member of the community. Normally it is the family's responsibility to toilet-train their child, teach him to feed himself, and teach him to say "please" and "thank you" at appropriate times. If a retarded child does not learn these things, there often is a strong community feeling that the parents are at fault, and sometimes parents even are discouraged from seeking preschool help until their children have acquired such skills.

A retarded child in a family that cannot cope with him, whatever the causes, generates pressure to separate him from the community (Wolfensberger, 1967). The social attitude tends to be either that his parents—which normally means his mother—must train him or that he must be placed

[3]We recognize the often overwhelming pressure that the presence of a retarded child creates in a family. See Chapter 10 for a discussion of it.

in a highly specialized training situation, which usually is translated to mean an institution. There is little public consideration of intermediate methods. If the parents have sufficient economic resources they may be able themselves to get outside help, or to organize or join a local association that will provide specialized help and yet let the child live at home. This solution, however, is not only expensive but fits only within the mores of the middle and upper clásses of society, where a mother has free time because she does not work and probably has enough help at home to care for her children.

Thus we find that local services consist of a number of health and welfare workers who usually are well qualified in their own areas but are inexperienced with retardation, of an overburdened school system, and of a family which has few ways of getting assistance or guidance. Together they produce some care, a lot of sympathy, but little effective help for the retarded.

In fact, we find that as a whole current services for retarded children leave a great deal to be desired. Community services, which offer the greatest hope, are not yet organized to do the job efficiently, and many communities do not even accept the idea that there is a job to be done. Institutions have become expensive disasters. It is clear there is an immediate need for a major shift in priorities throughout the country; the current management service models, no matter what the level, cannot provide reasonable solutions to the problems. There must be greater national emphasis on local facilities and a total rethinking of the role of the institutions; unless this is done we will continue to create more problems than we solve. But there is no good reason that our typical product should remain—as it is today—a disadvantaged child who starts out with a normal potential but ends up as a retarded person in an institution.

Part Two

Future Perspectives

In these fast-moving times it is difficult for authors to keep fully abreast of all developments in a field. Some of the problems underlined in Part One of this book have already been brought to the fore by way of court proceedings and public investigations. But it is not sufficient to underline and reveal problems. Changes must be sought.

Part Two, Future Perspectives, attempts to establish a theoretical and operational basis for modifying our attitudes and approaches to mental handicap. Both general and specific plans are offered. The more general are prototypic and obviously must be adjusted to the needs and resources of each of the states or communities. But the overall effort is to develop the kinds of programs that will permit the broadening of personal options and human rights.

The primary emphasis must be placed on the concept that all persons, regardless of the degree of handicap, can be helped. Further, many can also learn to help themselves. And it is our responsibility to give them the opportunities.

9

An Approach to Rehabilitation, Treatment and Training

It is unlikely that a retarded child ever will function in a completely normal way, but it is quite likely that his disability can be modified to make his handicaps much less visible. Rehabilitation consists of removing the barriers—whether they are adaptive, psychological, or social—that come between the child and effective, acceptance behavior (Leland & Goldberg, 1957). It is interesting to know what has caused the retarded condition, and sometimes we can recommend specific treatment, but it also may be completely irrelevant to the child's current behavior. What is relevant is the way this behavior relates to the demands of the child's personal environment.

Behavior Modification

Thus rehabilitation means reorganizing the child's response patterns or introducing new responses so that his general behavior is tolerable within his social setting. He already has developed response techniques and coping strategies; our problem centers on making them more acceptable. The most effective form of rehabilitation is behavior modification,[1] which is defined as "the application

[1]Those who wish a more detailed description of this approach should refer to the *Journal of Applied Behavior Analysis,* Lawrence, Kansas, 1970, Vol. I, and to Bricker (1970).

of behavior principles to the training and treatment of problem behavior in general" (Bijou, 1968, p. 985). Though these methods are comparatively new, there is now sufficient research to demonstrate that they are effective (Krasner & Ullman, 1965; Ullman & Krasner, 1965). Some of it has been highly specific, dealing with such matters as toilet training Giles & Wolfe, 1966) and some has been more general, dealing with broader areas such as personal responsibility (Ross, 1969).

Varying levels of retardation present varying forms of behavior to be modified; the approaches we use must be based on the child's priority needs. A highly specialized, carefully selected program must be devised for each child, to reverse his specific forms of unacceptable behavior. As a first step, we will place the child in one of three arbitrary categories: those severely and profoundly retarded, those moderately retarded, or those mildly retarded.

In the severely and profoundly retarded group, needs for changing the behavior center on self-help skills and primitive functioning. These are such matters as eating skills, toilet training and care of self at the toilet, dressing and undressing, washing and drying hands and face, brushing teeth, and similar activities (Bensberg, Colwell, & Cassell, 1965). They also include interpersonal activities such as mealtime behavior (Hendriksen & Doughty, 1967), responses to social stimuli (Hollis, 1965a, 1965b), as well as locomotive function, sensory development, and language acquisition.

Needs of the moderately retarded group also include some self-help skills; but chiefly they involve personal responsibility, decision making, motivation, and **self-concept.** In addition to such matters as use of eating utensils, dining in public, cleanliness and general appearance and care of clothing, children in this group should learn the use of the telephone, the handling of money, shopping skills, time and number concepts, kitchen and home duties, and the like. But the clinician also needs to consider work fitness, initiative, and other areas of responsibility and socialization. Modification training with this group includes both the use of socially valued behavior and the avoidance of socially costly behavior (Lent, LeBlanc, & Spradlin, 1967). The approaches include special techniques to improve the child's cooperation and his motivation for learning (Birnbrauer & Sawler, 1964; Birnbrauer, Bijou, Wolfe, & Kidder, 1965), and control of behavioral responses which interfere with skills already learned (Edwards & Lilly, 1966). Special demonstrations can be provided to help adults who work with such children learn to apply the proper techniques (Whitney & Bernard, 1966; Bensberg, 1965).

In the mildly or borderline retarded group, children mainly need correction of their reactions to social responsibility and their civic role. The greatest emphasis here is in social situations and structured experiences such as those in the classroom (Barrett, 1965, Barrett & Lindsley, 1962) and even in "natural life" settings (Tighe & Elliott, 1968). Efforts are made to enhance cognitive growth and develop normal social reactions. The focus is on such specifics as violent or destructive behavior, rebelliousness, untrustworthy behavior, withdrawal symptoms, old mannerisms, self-abusive behavior, sexually **aberrant** behavior, and other socially undesirable responses.

In each broad category, emphasis is not on the question of what forms of behavior can be modified, but rather on what forms *should* be modified. They are the ones that interfere with the child's ability to move to a higher level of functioning and acceptance. Once the forms that should be modified have been identified, priorities for behavioral changes can be worked out.

The decision as to which forms of behavior should be modified is based largely on social factors; the clinician must look at the social environment of the child and decide which activity is most required for him to survive. As an example, a severely retarded child who neither feeds nor dresses himself and who is not toilet-trained lacks three essential abilities. But the social milieu puts greater emphasis on toilet training than on the other two abilities, and it thus becomes the first priority for modification. On the other hand, if we are dealing with a very young child his social environment probably puts more emphasis on feeding than on toilet training, and so we would concentrate first upon his feeding problem. The child's family must be consulted and his sub-culture considered when these priorities are set up. As it is now possible to modify the expressed behavior or "field observable functioning," the individual can be helped to function within his social context even though some of the more basic etiological patterns have not been modified.

Training and Treatment

We must distinguish between training and treatment. Training is the introduction of new techniques, ideas, and information which the child does not yet possess. Treatment is the reordering or changing of already-held behavioral patterns or coping strategies to produce new strategies. In a training program we assume that the child has reached the level of physical and social development and that he is ready to be trained; that he is not avoiding the task of feeding himself, for instance, but rather that the methods used so far have been ineffective in showing him how to do it. But should it appear instead that he is actively avoiding the task, he then requires treatment before the training can begin.

There are many ways in which training can be provided. Among them are training programs associated with special education, preschools, and day care centers; training programs found in comprehensive community mental retardation centers and sheltered workshops; training programs in residential institutions; demonstration projects within large MR centers; and many supportive training programs such as camping or more adult recreational activities. All of these must focus on shaping positive forms of behavior that can be substituted for those forms that are unacceptable socially.

Training intended to modify behavior is generally based on combining the more traditional concepts of reward and punishment with newer elements where the concept of avoidance of pain, interference, or discomfort is taught (Premack, 1965). This latter concept is established on the principle that the person will proceed along chosen lines, but will modify his road if it is blocked in order to avoid the interference which has been created. Thus various non-aversive types of punishment may be used if they are conceived by the patient as punishing, and he will modify his behavior voluntarily in order to avoid these interferences. A child in his natural home environment usually will be rewarded by his parents for his typical daily activity; his mother may give him a second helping of dessert or some other favorite food or buy small items she knows will please him, while his father may pick him up and hug him or go out and play ball with him. He receives a constant flow of pennies, nickels, and general privileges such as staying up to see a special television show or being taken to a movie. Thus the adults in his environment tend to create a variable-interval reward pattern that quite often is not directly contingent upon his accomplishments, but that reinforces his general positive behavior.

When the child is brought into a community or institutional program, he finds that he must do things which he was not doing at home—perhaps even things that he refused to do or could not do. At one time under these circumstances there was a tendency to expect a child to do whatever he had been trained to do in the program and to punish him if he did not do it; he was not given any of the rewards that children at home usually receive as a matter of course. Now, however, most such training programs also use the typical reward procedures of a normal home. The rewards reinforce culturally desirable behavior, but even so, they have been attacked by some critics as bribes. It is surely unfortunate that a second helping, which a child would expect as a member of a loving family, is looked upon as a bribe once he is in an institution. No institution, regardless of how well managed it may be, can really place a child in a normal environment; to minimize the dehumanizing factors inherent to such an establishment, it is important to give some special rewards that favor the child.

Further, the educational and daily living processes should be treated as though they were part of the child's work day, and he should be paid for carrying them out as an adult would be paid for his work. Payment for the child, however, is in the form of tokens that have value for him (Girardeau & Spradlin, 1964). Work activities for such a child consist of the wide variety of things he should be encouraged to do. These may include dressing neatly, not sitting and watching television when he should be outside playing with others, or actually working in the form of making a bed or ironing a blouse. They may simply consist of being pleasant all day, or smiling on occasion, or behaving properly on the playground. And they may also include progress in academic subjects. But whatever the activities may be, they are modifications of undesirable forms of behavior; the token rewards for correct behavior can then be converted into true rewards that have meaning for the child. He can buy special privileges, he can buy personal time for special activities, or he can buy material things such as toys and candy.

Should the child fail to do the appointed tasks he does not receive payment, as is true in most work situations; if the failure is gross enough, a certain amount is docked from his holdings. If he chooses to spend his earnings in buying swear words, or a dirty shirt, or television time when he should be elsewhere, the tokens are removed and he is not able to buy candy or other desirable things with them. In this way an economy is set up which enables the child to develop a self-concept, a feeling that he is part of something real, and an understanding that part of his survival is based on his behavior and that he has some control of the outcome.

The younger child and the more seriously retarded child have a greater need for more immediate, direct rewards with less emphasis on tokens; both of them will find it hard to conceive of abstract ideas such as the tokens represent, or to delay rewards and still relate them to the required task. As a child grows older or his level of functioning improves, more abstractions can be introduced into his program. At first the teacher must rely heavily on reinforcement by rewards and on punishment by nonstringent methods; basically they are means of communication between the teacher and the child who is being trained. Once the child gains clear recognition of cues, many of these training reinforcements can be dropped, for the tasks then begin to develop their own social reinforcement and the rewards tend to be more a matter of praise than of anything else.

Much of the training depends on imitation (Baer & Sherman, 1965; Baer, Peterson, & Sherman, 1967). As the child shifts more to social rewards and social reinforcement, there is also a shift to place greater emphasis on following the patterns set by adult models. The child then is encouraged to learn independently how to cope with a variety of situations; this is done by giving him the chance to cope successfully in a limited environment where he can test his ability to modify and control his behavior. With less-retarded individuals this process can become quite effective in helping them learn to deal with social situations on a broad scale. It will give them coping skills that enable them to modify their behavior in new situations and thus perhaps handle the new problems successfully. Such a child should also be trained to seek guidance in times of stress; if he is unable to cope he can then still postpone a serious decision until he can get help.

Language and Cognition

It should be emphasized that man is a language-bearing animal and that he is the only animal in whom there is cognition above the most rudimentary processes (Lenneberg, 1967). These concepts should be included in all techniques used for behavior modification. Severely and profoundly retarded youngsters have a very limited ability to understand the complexities of language, and will need other forms of communication; but higher functioning children have more tools available to them and can deal with higher language functions.

And a retarded child must be required to use all of the tools that he has. The process of "forcing the child to think" (Leland & Smith, 1965) is part of the behavior modification scheme. The child must also know what he has done and what has been done to him if there are to be efficient results. For example, if he is photographed on TV walking in the typical shuffle of the retardate and then sees both this tape and those of people walking with a vigorous stride, he will observe his errors and be able to copy the stride. Repeated pictures will enable him to see the changes in his own performance and appreciate his gains.

Another process is the development of skills in prototype television programs using the "Captain Kangaroo" format. The child earns the right to be on TV and to talk with "Captain" or his "rabbit" by having performed certain tasks such as combing his hair or being friendly. Thus a reward system can be based on privileges earned (Toombs, 1967).

A variation of this approach with higher functioning patients is to tape groups who are in round-table discussions on real problems of daily living—the equivalent of student government meetings. The children gain experience not only through participation in decision making but also by watching playbacks of the session on closed-circuit television. In this type of training it is essential that whatever decisions are reached by the group are actually carried out and that they then exercise final judgment on the consequences.

There are a number of training approaches for specific and readily identifiable needs, such as reading particular words or writing the child's name. Among them are the Rainier Reading Program (Bijou, Birnbrauer, Kidder, & Tague, 1966), the Peabody Language Development Program (American Guidance Service, 1970), and more generalized approaches to programmed learning in a variety of educational skills (Haring & Phillips, 1962). Such approaches have also been designed for advanced phases of vocational rehabilitation and job training (Crosson, 1969; Crosson, Youngberg, & White, 1970), perceptual understanding and sensory responses (Frostig & Horne, 1965), and other specific functions.

The workers who evolved these programs used many of the features suggested by Maria Montessori and other pioneers in the use of **developmental milestones.** (A developmental milestone is the accomplishment of a necessary growth state—one that represents a building block for the next stage.) This learning approach develops a step-by-step process which picks up these milestones wherever possible, even though their application may be delayed because of the retardation of the individual. It is a particularly useful approach in social training, such as can be done at summer camp or community recreation centers (Pumphrey & Peters, 1969) and during leisure activities (Shellhaas, 1969a; 1969b) or in the child's home.

Part of the technique uses repetition in the motor areas involved and combinations of the senses. The child is taught how **sense experience**—touch, smell, hearing, and sight—all provide stimuli, and all of the stimuli are used to reinforce his learning (Robinson & Robinson, 1965). If the problem at hand is teaching a child to button his clothing, he should be given time to feel the button and the buttonhole, to put the button into his mouth if he wishes (although he should be protected against swallowing it), and to understand that this object is a regular part of his environment. Then he should begin putting the button through the buttonhole, first on a Montessori button board, then on his own clothing.

More complicated tasks can be taught in a similar manner. If a child is being trained to tell time, a clock should be used that has numbers of felt or sandpaper that can be touched; they should also make a noise when they are touched and possibly a light should go on, so that there are cues involving feeling, hearing, and sight. After the child can report major time units (hours, half hours, and quarter hours) these should be related to meaningful events such as meals, television shows, or a parent's return from work. The transfer to a real clock is made after these associations become fixed. This kind of training can often be worked out at home, and should be.

Social perceptual training for moderate to borderline retarded can be given in somewhat the same way. The child is placed in structured situations where the trainer knows the logical outcome and where he can help the child to draw inferences and make predictions, to read social cues, and to evolve coping skills. Successful experiences here will provide the training steps that enable the child to approach new situations with more liklihood of success, even though he has not had previous experience with their exact counterparts. To accomplish this he must during the training period have direct contact with social perceptual problems in which he is required to draw major inferences in order to participate in the activities involved (Edmonson, deJung, Leland, &

Leach, 1971). As training progresses he should be encouraged to strive for a more adult level of interaction and to test his social performance in such matters as dating activities and interviews with potential employers. This sort of training will put a finish on all of the previous work done with the child in the area of independent functioning and will enable him to make the best use of all the aspects of social and personal responsibility that he has learned (MacLeech, 1968).

The other aspect of behavior modification is treatment. Many patients have forms of behavior that are personally or socially maladaptive. These forms are considered pathological, not because they are exhibited by the retarded but because they are anti-social, negative, or hostile aspects that place the individual at war with society in addition to his retardation. Often these aspects of behavior must be modified before training can begin. The child already has coping strategies or behavioral patterns, but they must be reshaped into acceptable forms.

Thus the child who constantly defecates at the side of a building can be induced to defecate in the bathroom. The child who constantly uses foul language can be brought to use the same speech mechanism in a socially acceptable manner. The child who constantly hits other children can be led to express his hostility in other ways. But if the child's repertoire of behavior is so deficient that there is nothing there to be reshaped, then we must turn first to methods of training rather than treatment. In this way programs of training and of treatment support each other. They should not be separated artificially, and certainly every good therapist does a certain amount of training. But in overall terms, if the goal is to correct anti-social symptoms, the emphasis is placed on treatment; if the goal is to improve the learning of information then the emphasis is placed on training.

The Emotionally Disturbed Retarded

There are retarded individuals who are also emotionally disturbed (Gittelman & Birch, 1967), a condition that often manifests itself in hostile or destructive behavior. Typically this behavior is so completely unacceptable socially that the person cannot survive in any normal setting; its forms range from public sexual acts to self-mutilation and head-banging. Such individuals may have any degree of retardation and thus may be found at all functional levels. A number of approaches are used to treat these patients. Some of the approaches are lumped under the general term of "behavior therapy" (Bandura, 1967; Grossberg, 1964) and are conceived as clinical programs designed to handle specific symptoms. Usually they punish the child for exhibiting the symptoms, at times using extreme forms of aversive stimuli such as high-voltage electric shocks (Wolpe & Lazarus, 1966) and at times using a series of lesser aversive stimuli that lead systematically toward avoidance of pain to improve behavior (Doubros, 1966). The hope is that the child will abandon the symptomatic behavior and develop new forms of behavior (Baller, 1956).

A therapist using such an approach may be very successful in correcting specific symptoms, but he probably then will find considerable difficulty in arranging conditions that allow development of desirable behavior. One way this can be done is to set up environmental situations in a **"play therapy"** approach that permit modification of the anti-social behavior and that also give the child a number of alternative choices. If he selects a choice that is acceptable he is permitted to continue and is thus rewarded (Leland & Smith, 1965). If, however, the therapist does not approve of this alternate behavior he then intrudes and blocks or punishes the child for making the wrong choice. This method keeps the concept of reward and punishment (Gardner, W., 1969), but helps the child learn to choose and test alternative situations. The experience he gains here can be transferred later to situations where the therapist is not present but where there are parallel coping demands (Leland & Smith, 1972).

A similar approach to a much less drastic form of treatment is found in activities of occupational, recreational, and music therapists, and also in those of speech and physical therapists who have more specific goals. Behavior modification and shaping are used by all of these people to develop a self-concept in the child and help to give him a feeling of success and reward as a result of acceptable behavior in public activities. The therapists' main purpose here is to use the child's skills and techniques as a means to modify his behavior. For example, if he can be taught to interact with an occupational therapist in a friendly, confident way, because he appreciates her help with the ashtray he is making, she can use this **rapport** to establish a more complicated social relationship. Then should he become angry and break the ashtray, the therapist can express her displeasure so that he understands that he has damaged their relationship and made her unhappy, and that if he is to work with the clay again he must in some way make amends.

To accomplish this the therapist must intervene actively to make the patient realize that he has broken something, that he has displeased her, and that she is very unhappy about the situation. If he is earning credit points or other reinforcement devices, some of them can be deducted because of his action and this will then be considered as making amends; the child has paid for what he has done and things can start over again. But if there is no tangible element involved, the child should be expected to clear up the situation on the social level by some sort of personally responsible action; this may not occur until the next occupational therapy session when he may come in smiling or making a friendly gesture toward the therapist as a way of asking that things start over. There is not a demand for a formal apology, but the child must indicate in some way that he realizes what he did. In such circumstances the withholding of friendship can become a mighty element of punishment and should be utilized to correct destructive behavior. Under no conditions should destructive behavior be accepted as though it were normal or unimportant, for then the child will also feel that it is unimportant and he will make no progress.

Psychotherapy can also be quite effective with the mentally retarded (Bialer, 1967; Leland & Smith, 1965). Here again the treatment should not be oriented toward etiology but rather to changing unacceptable behavior. There are no specific defects that in themselves lead to pathological acts, and so treatment must address the behavior itself. The general approach is to gain rapport with the patient and then, through a variety of methods, to find the key to his behavior. After that it becomes relatively simple to get him to modify it.

Severely and profoundly retarded children lack communication facility and thus do not respond readily to traditional therapeutic approaches. With them, treatment processes must place greater emphasis on intrusion and corrective control than they do with less severely retarded patients (Cowan, Hoddinott, & Wright, 1965; Hamilton, Stephens, & Allen, 1967). Conversely, moderately retarded children display many cognitive elements and thus can respond to **activity therapy,** play therapy, and similar approaches as well as to some of the more traditional forms of psychotherapy (Bialer, 1967).

But no matter what the level of retardation or the form of treatment, all retarded individuals have one factor in common. Before they can be trained to function in society at an acceptable level they must first conceive of themselves as viable people. They must know that they can be responsible for their own behavior; that things do not just happen to them but that they themselves make many of the events happen as a result of their own actions; that despite obvious functional differences they can still approach some situations with expectations of success. This is as true of the profoundly retarded child who eventually learns to feed himself as of the mildly retarded one who finds a job and is absorbed into society with expectation of a reasonably normal future.

The Overall Plan

Any behavior modification plan will combine treatment and training. It will emphasize the reversal of those forms of behavior that can be reversed and the shaping of those which, if they cannot be reversed, can be sufficiently modified to make them less unpleasant and more acceptable. As a result of the plan, the total status of the individual will improve; both his own self-concept and his social abilities will be better. He then will begin to see that potentially he may have a role to play in the total social environment and that—particularly if he is not too severely retarded—he can perform much as he sees his peers performing.

This is not to imply that the total handicap will vanish. A child will be just as handicapped when he finishes such a program as he was when he went into it. Nothing in the program will induce the growing of a new brain, but the subject will have learned various ways of coping with his deficiencies so that they will not be a permanent block to more normal functioning. The severely and profoundly retarded person may still need long periods of residential care and he may still not be able to function readily at home in a way that fits into the pattern of family life. We can expect no miracles, but we can help the patient develop his maximum abilities to do certain things for himself.

10

A Mentally Retarded Child in the Family

The interaction of a retarded child with his family is both more intense and more prolonged than if he were normal. As a result his parents need a great deal of help. They have problems in recognizing and accepting the child's handicaps and they need counseling on the day-to-day situations that surround him and his normal brothers and sisters (Robinson & Robinson, 1965).

Parents who want to keep a retarded child at home may find themselves under great pressures to do otherwise. They often are made to feel that somehow they are neglecting him by not giving him the opportunities that supposedly would be available in an institution; such pressures may originate with schools and school counselors who decide that the child's problems center around parents who do not understand or who do not want to cooperate. At times there almost seems to be a feeling that it is unfortunate the child has parents (Wright, 1960, p. 290).

In applying these pressures to the parents, well-meaning people often cite stereotypes or cliches about the effect of a retarded child on normal siblings or on the social or job situation of the father. But in fact, there is very little real evidence about the complexities of these relationships (Farber, 1968). Discussion of the child and his family

The authors wish to thank Antionette Cyrulik-Jacobs, M.A., University of Wisconsin, for helping to develop the main lines of this chapter.

involves evident variables. The child's condition can range from mild to profound; the family's stability and its ability to handle problems can range from weak to strong. Thus every case is unique and it is impossible to generalize about such effects.

In actuality the family can be a major resource for work with a retarded child. They can help keep the child out of an institution, they can develop skills or talents within the child in conjunction with other programs, and they can function as a part of any treatment and training program necessary. Instead of this being the first resource used, however, typically it is ignored until all others have failed.

It is true that a retarded child's problem can reflect or even be caused in part by family problems and parental reactions (Johnson, 1963). The retarded child is as much a mirror of his family as a normal child, and if parents cannot solve the problems generated by having him in the family the consequences can be severe. But not all parents find the problem insurmountable, and even those who initially do, often can be helped to surmount them. It is so much better for a child to remain with his family that removing him should be considered a last resort, not a routine first move as is now so often the case.

Parental Reactions to the Child

Parental reactions seem to fall into certain patterns, regardless of the nature of the handicap. As a result, a good deal is known about their reactions and it is not difficult to determine what they are in a given case and then take steps to alleviate them. Most family problems in this area originate in usual, everyday situations; it is the parents' lack of understanding that usually creates the confusion. There is a tendency for a family to close in on itself when it has a retarded child and to center so closely on the child that it itself becomes what might be called a handicapped family. But most parents can readily work their way through the problems if they have the opportunity to share the situation through parent groups or associations (Zwerling, 1954) or through counseling and guidance from professionals experienced in this area (McDonald, 1962).

The parents probably share most of society's standard responses to retardation—revulsion, fear, avoidance, curiosity, and various superstitious feelings—and yet this is *their* baby. The resulting conflict often produces a reaction of denial, saying that somewhere, somehow, some mistake has been made. The extremes of this pattern are the parents who accuse the hospital of mixing up babies and giving them the wrong one.

Commonly the reaction of denial is followed by a rather lengthy period of "chronic sorrow" (Olshansky, 1966). It combines elements of hopelessness and self-pity, genuine sympathy for the child, and mourning for the child they expected but did not receive (Farber, 1960). This latter feeling at times may be so strong that the expected child is mourned as a lost member of the family and the actual child is rejected without any recognition that he is very much their child and vitally needs their help (Mandelbaum & Wheeler, 1960). In extreme cases this may even lead to moves to institutionalize the child shortly after birth or as soon as the institution will accept him—an action that should not be taken except for the most extreme medical reasons. Such early institutionalization is psychologically destructive to the child; if it is attempted, the social work department or other appropriate people in the facility should be certain that the parents understand all the implications and should encourage them to keep and enjoy the baby unless his survival depends upon removal.

The initial parental responses can be controlled if the physician attending at the birth takes immediate steps to get counseling for the parents as soon as the child's handicap is known. In severe cases the condition can be recognized almost at birth, particularly if the nurses are aware of the reactions they should be looking for, such things as low **APGAR** (Apgar, 1953) rating (showing that vital signs are missing or delayed), and are alert to the possible absence of other expected reactions. There should be counseling services immediately available so that the parents are helped to understand and begin to control their reactions even before mother and child leave the hospital. Mildly retarded children probably will not be identified until they enter school, but then there should be the same immediate counseling available. The local physician or other person to whom the family turns for advice should realize that his responsibilities include the obtaining of counseling for the parents as soon as possible (Kanner, 1953a).

Parental Adjustment to the Child

Although some families never progress beyond these initial grief reactions, if they are basically strong or if they receive adequate help parents normally advance into a transitional stage of adjustment. There will still be feelings of loss for the child that was supposed to be, and usually little understanding of the potential in the child that is. But the parents make some adjustment to the fact that they have a child with a very serious problem and they develop some recognition of the problem in its own terms. They have, in effect, come to know that the child is handicapped and that there are many things he cannot do, though they still may not recognize that there are many things he *can* do. This transitional period is typically associated with much soul searching and seeking for possible causes, and is often associated with much personal guilt, with the parents saying "if I had only eaten such-and-such a thing" or "if I had not done such-and-such a thing" this would not have happened. The personal guilt may also be blamed on the opposite parent, by saying "there never was anything like this in my family; this must come from your family."

Throughout this period of searching the parents are continually plagued by feelings of guilt and worry. Sometimes the explanations they make as to the cause of the handicap resemble dark-age mythology. The mother did not have "the right influences" during pregnancy, or she was scared by an animal, or the fates were against her, or she wanted a baby so desperately that she was given this one as her "cross to bear," or conversely, she was so happy with the pregnancy that "people do not deserve to be that happy" and she had to pay for her joy. It is at this stage that a family may burn itself out in trying to deal with the intense feelings of confusion caused by its retarded child, and the child may have to be removed from the family to alleviate the situation.

More typically, however, the transitional reactions are just what the name implies—short-lived and a bridge to a healthier pattern in which parents begin to accept the situation, take a solid look at the new child, and try to understand the nature and extent of his handicap.

Unfortunately there still is a tendency on the part of some physicians to tell the parents to wait, because the child will outgrow the problem. This may be true in a biological sense (most retarded children do outgrow their specific, infantile biological symptoms), but it overlooks the fact that early intervention may help the child. Worse, it creates a do-nothing kind of hope. More important, it leaves a Sword of Damocles hanging over the parents, and places them in a highly difficult situation, always wondering when the day will come that their child will be normal; and finally they grow aware that he never will be.

Knowledge of the relative seriousness of the problem usually comes in one of two ways. Either the parents are informed by a doctor, social worker, or some other professional person, or they reach the conclusion through their own observation. If they receive appropriate guidance at this point they can begin to plan and to form realistic hopes (Wright, 1960). It often is a mistake for counselors to give too much reassurance or comfort, however, because it may be misunderstood, particularly if there was a previous period of false hope. Rather, the counselor must work toward awareness of reality, which sometimes may be quite harsh.

A profoundly retarded child may be less of a problem than one who has moderate or mild retardation, for his situation is more clear-cut and residential care may be the only adequate solution. The less retarded child presents different types of problems which often depend on the socioeconomic level of the parents. Middle-class parents see mild to moderate retardation as a much greater problem than do poverty-group parents because their expectations for their children are much greater and because there is a greater feeling of competition among middle-class families (Veblen, 1934). Where expectations are only for continued poverty, a child unable to rise socially still will be living at the expected level (Lewis, 1966).

Part of the self-image of middle-class people in terms of family responsibility demands that they do everything they possibly can for their child. Typically they make a highly conscientious effort to understand his condition in order to seek answers. Poorer parents are very cooperative if they receive guidance which makes them a part of the intervention procedures (Wolfe, Giles, & Hall, 1968), but their lack of resources leads them to feel that they can do nothing about the situation themselves and therefore seek out someone who can (*Spearhead at Juniper Gardens,* 1968). More affluent parents, however, will attempt to solve their own problems.

Search for Solutions

As their awareness of the situation increases, parents are likely to begin a new search for solutions, and often this takes the form of multiple professional consultations. The professionals may be well-qualified people or they may be faith-healers or quacks who offer quick (and very expensive) cures which the parents out of desperation buy. Even if the parents stay with ethical, qualified professionals, they may become involved in what can be described as a game of "musical doctors"—going from one source to another in search of a definite, specific solution which does not exist, or hoping to find someone who will say that nothing is wrong and everything will eventually turn out all right (McDonald, 1962).

This concept of shopping may be motivated by the lack of confidence the parents have for professionals in general, but more often it is brought on by a deliberate vagueness on the part of the professional persons, either because of their own lack of experience with mental retardation or their own lack of faith in the reliability of their answers, regardless of their experience.

The parents have a tendency to expect to come away with a prescription which will cause some sort of immediate response. Even when the professional person is highly expert in the area of mental retardation and able to speak with some degree of assurance, he is not going to provide this kind of remedy and the parents come away from the consultation without material evidence of having been there. This leads them to feel that the doctor has not done anything (even though he may have given very important advice or consultation concerning diet, behavior, or other matters) and so, many times the parents will continue to shop in the hope that there will be a doctor who can deal with the problem.

The question of treatment often leads to intra-family conflict, with the parents accusing each other of not really loving the child or not wanting to do the best for him. The pressure of the problem, especially with more severely or profoundly retarded children, can bring turmoil and dispair; parents may begin to lose sight of each other by over-devoting to the child and break up the family in the process (Nichols, *Joe Egg,* 1967; Liberthson, 1968). The constant demands of the handicapped child may also keep his brothers and sisters from receiving proper attention and this generates additional family strains. Various forms of non-medical therapy ranging from speech therapy to psychotherapy will contribute to the emotional well-being of the child and thus of his family (Boston, 1960), but these are complicated, expensive, and may require from one to three years of continuous therapeutic intervention. Often an institution becomes the only answer to save the family from bankruptcy and to keep the rest of its members together (Mercer, 1966; Kershner, 1970).

Development of a Family Plan

If parents are to keep a retarded child successfully at home, one of the first things they must develop is an integrated family plan. They must learn as much as possible about the problem, not through the emotionally driven shopping tours of doctors' offices, but by seeking out the best experts in their geographic area and obtaining guidance as to the actions they should take, the available literature dealing with their problems, and the names of other parents who have similar children and with whom they can compare experiences (Zwerling, 1954). There must be enough discussion with clinicians and other parents that these parents begin to comprehend what part of their child's behavior is normal for his period of growth and what part is really symptomatic of his handicap.

Parents seldom attain full acceptance of the child (Kanner, 1953a) in the sense of appreciating his individuality, having some pride in his assets, and tolerating his shortcomings, but the extent to which they can approach these goals often determines the degree of stability and happiness he can achieve. The family situation is difficult and is likely to be characterized on the part of the child by high degrees of frustration and personal periods of fear, guilt, and anger; and on the part of the other family members by continued feelings of doubt as to whether they have made the right decisions and are doing the right thing. Parents can usually reach an intellectual understanding of the problem, but it is much more difficult for them to accept it emotionally.

The parents are highly vulnerable to the opinions of friends and relatives, yet those same friends and relatives will tend to follow the parents' lead in their reactions to the child. Thus if other people reject or do not tolerate the child, the parents will find difficulty in giving him the warmth and affection he needs; yet when they appear negative and withdrawn from him, others will follow their pattern. Generally friends and neighbors will not know how to approach the child and will suppose that the parents know best; so if they are warm and loving, others will be more apt to react in the same way. Further, the child probably will respond in the manner that he is expected to; but the parents clearly first have to set the scene. Only a very open and honest kind of interaction can maintain any kind of family unity. Otherwise the family will be approached by others with suspicion and even fear, and the parents' other children may lose their friends and develop atypical life styles (Farber, 1969; 1968).

Meeting and Dealing with Family Problems

Even after the family has made some adjustment to his presence, the practical problems surrounding the child with more serious handicaps may take their toll of family relationships. Financial matters invariably become a point of contention, for the child may require extra medical care, drugs, special diets, prosthetic devices, and care of the additional illnesses to which such children have a predisposition. It will be difficult for parents or siblings to entertain at home. Relationships with neighbors may be strained because of the child's behavior at play. The constant supervision and care required by the child keep the parents from pursuing many desirable leisure-time activities and prevent them from living a normal life outside the home. Day-to-day care of the child requires extreme patience, control, and sacrifice on the part of the parents, although sometimes the responsibilities are passed on to an older brother or sister who may give up all outside social contacts and tend to withdraw into the home. It is not surprising that in the face of these complex problems families seldom achieve full acceptance of the child and often utilize the institution as a way of saving the family (Mercer, 1966).

When a family decides to keep a child, however, there sometimes develops a tendency to think of him as the center of all family ills. If his father loses his job or a brother breaks his leg, somehow it is the fault of a retarded child. This kind of rejection is worse than the physical rejection of sending the child away, because under these circumstances there is no place to which he can escape and he becomes more retarded, more emotionally confused and disturbed, and more apt to become dangerous to himself and perhaps others.

Families who have a moderately handicapped child face other difficulties. Often he looks quite normal and people around him expect him to respond normally. When he does not, they may tease him or react in other ways that indicate they think nothing is actually wrong with him, and as a result he may come to be considered stupid rather than handicapped. The parents may not realize what the problem is—or even that there is a problem—until the child enters school and they find that he has difficulty in keeping up with the work or in interacting with other children. If they have had some realization that there was a problem they may either have become overly defensive about the child or have openly derided him for being stupid. But whether or not they had previous clues, when they are told as a diagnostic fact that he is retarded, many parents consider it a personal insult and react negatively both toward the school and toward the child, approaching him as though he were lazy and somehow bringing the whole problem upon himself.

Even though in due time the family probably will become better adjusted to the fact that there is a real mental handicap present, they may still find it difficult to identify the specific areas of handicap, particularly since with the mildly retarded these center around factors of personal responsibility and decision making. They know that the child cannot be trusted in many decision-making situations, but they are not always sure just what these are or when they may develop. The undercurrent of mistrust that develops sets up constant feelings of tension and the child typically becomes very angry in the face of his family. Social interactions outside the family are also difficult, because the child looks normal and is expected by others to function normally in social situations. Parents who have a mildly or moderately retarded older girl may become much alarmed because they feel she is easy prey to aggressive males who will take advantage of her inability to make appropriate decisions.

Such retarded children function well enough to want to participate in the social activities of their normal brothers or sisters, but not well enough to be welcome there. This provides an additional source of conflict, especially if there is a retarded older child who is not permitted to do certain things his younger brother or sister may do.

But on the other hand, the mildly or moderately retarded child fits into the overall family situation much more adequately than does the more seriously retarded one. He can and should be expected to do many things for himself. These things, however, fall into the area of independent functioning rather than specific intellectual performance, and this must be understood if the child is not to be constantly placed in frustrating situations. The family has to find those activities that can reinforce the child's self-concept. At times such activities may be something they can be proud of, such as artistic or athletic achievements. The main difficulty the parents have is that they must constantly say, "I know my child looks normal, but he does not act normal"—rarely in those specific words, but with the thought always in mind.

The adjustment of such a child centers upon the level of his adaptive behavior. If he has developed maladaptive patterns in relationship to social responsibility, the family will need considerable help and support in modifying his behavior, at times even to the extent of an intensive intervention program. But if the behavior can be modified, there is a good probability that a mildly retarded individual can become a contributing member of society who does not have too many emotional problems.

The level of retardation is not as important as society's attitude. If we can accept the fact that children in difficulty need help and that there are groups of children with certain types of developmental learning defects who need special help, it does not really matter how much help they need.

Continuing Dependency

All such individuals probably will have some form of continuing dependency. They will have to have continuous and general contact with more able members of society in order to deal with those aspects of their physical and personal needs with which their defects interfere. The epileptic individual needs neurological and medical follow-up to keep his **anticonvulsant** medication regulated and to permit him to maintain some level of personal control. The child with motoric dysfunctions may need a helper to deal with elements in the environment that would otherwise make locomotion impossible. Even if he is in a wheelchair (whether or not he can move it himself), there still will be many areas for which he will need some sort of help—stairs, high curbs, crowds, etc. Deaf and blind children need both medical and psychological support, and again there are vast areas within the normal environment with which they will not be able to cope unless they have additional help. If they are mentally retarded in addition to their special defects, the continuing dependency will be very great. But even in those retarded persons without special defects this continuing dependency will emerge because of their underlying difficulty in making appropriate decisions and in dealing with the cues of the surrounding environment. Thus, those who are functioning at a level lower than that which society is ready to accept are individuals who have a continuing need for regular follow-up throughout their development. Both the family and the community are involved with a highly complicated interaction over a long number of years concerning these continuing dependency needs.

Here the concept of cure has to be totally rejected. One cannot say that the individual has received certain treatment and therefore is ready to go into the world without further help. Society has recognized this to the extent of institutionalizing individuals who need regular twenty-four-hour supervision. For those who do not need intensive residential care it is obviously more appropriate to provide agencies which can be available from time to time as they are needed, rather than the extremely expensive process of twenty-four-hour-a-day, and three-hundred-sixty-five-days-a-year institutionalization.

Home training programs are particularly desirable to introduce specialists in child development and special education into the home when the retarded child is still at preschool level.[1] The resources of the home trainer can help the parents begin to reverse those forms of behavior that will make the child most visible socially (Lindsley, 1966). The home trainer also can help the parents. They become aware through this process that people are more accepting than might be expected and that if the child can maintain some level of behavioral control, most people will not even know he is around. They learn that the feelings of others often are reflections of their own feelings. And above all, they learn that their child is not the only one of his kind in the community. Thus the home trainer becomes in many respects an addition to the family instead of an invader, someone who permits the family to develop an appropriate program at a time when the child needs it most. A mutually dependent relationship is developed between the child, his family, and the outward community, and this

[1]Parents interested in such programs should contact their local State Department of Special Education or their local unit of the Association for Retarded Children.

interdependency becomes very rewarding to all who share in it (Robinson & Robinson, 1965).

When a parent of a child with moderate or mild retardation begins to respond to the rewards of his child's growth and development there is a strong tendency to feel that he possibly could become normal. The concept of **"normalization"** has received a great deal of general attention; and a retarded child does share many of the typical patterns of growth and development associated with all children. Retarded children have many requirements in common with normal children: they get hungry, they get thirsty, they get hurt, they use many of the same strategies to cope with these things. As they grow older they have a need for love and affection, which will lead to real friendships (MacAndrew & Edgerton, 1966) and may eventually blossom into strong emotional ties and even marriage. Certainly one must give the retarded person every opportunity to respond as a normal person would under similar circumstances; but also the reality of his handicap must be kept firmly in mind.

There are permanent aspects of retardation that will limit a normal life in important ways. Planning by the parents must take into consideration both the good and the bad aspects of the situation; true acceptance of the problem by the family includes sincere understanding of both. For example, it should be understood that the child ought to have a school experience in conjunction with normal children, but that he will not be able to read as they do; that he ought to interact with children in games, but that sometimes he will gain more if they are children younger than he is; that he must have social contacts with members of both sexes, but that he will always need some help in working out his relationships with them. If these and similar matters are understood, then the parents can make appropriate plans for him to have an independent existence of his own.

As the child grows older he will need resources outside the family, perhaps the help of a dentist, a social worker, or some other person experienced in working with people who have this type of handicap. In every community or group of rural communities there should be a place where he can turn for this help. Ideally it might be a club that rents rooms, has recreational facilities (similar to those of the early YMCA's), has a desk clerk who is a trained community service worker, and has arrangements for social workers, nurses, and other specialists to be available on call. The retarded person would be a member of the club and his membership card would identify him to police or others whom he might meet in emergencies; it could also contain information about any medication he required and other pertinent facts. The club or center would be available to retarded people or their families whenever it was needed. Such needs could range from ten minutes of advice about making a purchase to extensive consultation regarding the problems of a possible marriage. Society should recognize that a part of its population needs more help and services than the rest, and it should provide a way of getting them, on a **"lifetime planning"** basis (see Chapter 12).

In the long run the situation will change from that of a family with a retarded child to that of a retarded adult in a family that will eventually disappear as the parents die and the children move off on their own. This problem must be anticipated realistically to avoid the extreme tragedy of having to institutionalize a thirty- or forty-year-old man who has lived at home all his life. The major aspect of the planning is to be certain that there are alternate emotional and personal resources for the retarded individual so that when the family does break up he will not be isolated, but will have friends and resources of his own, and perhaps his own family.

Possible solutions for a retarded adult as his family passes from the scene depend upon his level of handicap and his ability to do things for himself. Higher-level retarded individuals whose earlier relationship has been sound and properly planned will be in a better position to be left alone and will develop their own relationships and find other resources (Katz, 1968). The more severely retarded person who has lived with his parents may best be put in a nursing home or a retirement home if there is no one else to guide him and care for him. Whenever it is at all possible, such a person should not be required to go into an institution so late in his life.

The family must forsee that eventually the retarded person will have to survive without them, and they must do everything possible to help him learn to function independently so that such a drastic step as institutionalization need never occur. They must in some way arrange for an environmental pattern in the future that will be similar to the one he has left. If the training of the retarded person during his childhood placed the highest priority on the functions necessary for his survival, there should be no undue worry about him in his old age.

The Retarded Family

The discussion of a retarded child in a normal family and of his adjustment to life after his parents no longer can care for him brings us to the **retarded family**—a family in which husband, wife, or both are retarded.

In the most typical of such arrangements only one of the members is retarded, most often the female. This is particularly true in the lower socioeconomic levels, where a moderately or mildly retarded girl without major physical disabilities is an acceptable sex object and partner to males who are normal but often at the lower end of the intellectual scale. The parents of such girls can see to their futures rather effectively by arranging for their marriage. Quite often this move produces a thoroughly adequate family relationship, and if the girl has elemental housekeeping skills and an ability to maintain warmth and affection for her husband, the new family may be highly successful. The fact that the retarded girl can find in marriage a socially acceptable answer to her problems probably accounts for the fact that most institutions for the retarded have twice as many male as female residents (AAMD, 1968).

The problem becomes greater if both members of the family are retarded, because there is then no one who can make the important decisions. Sometimes a grandparent or other person may assume the guardianship of such a family by maintaining their budget and watching over them at crucial times, but more often there is no one to help. The couple must then function at their own level. One of them may gain and hold an unskilled job quite successfully. They are the people who first lose their jobs during periods of unemployment, however, but they become known to welfare workers and somehow survive.

It is interesting that at times their survival becomes a matter of community interaction at the lowest level; groups of retarded people may come together with alcoholics, narcotic addicts, and other social outcasts in the worst areas of a town, all banding together and depending on each other for mutual survival (Gorki [1903] 1964). If the whole community could only adopt a similar attitude toward the need for survival of all its members, the situation could be much improved. Retarded families, in particular, are usually more than willing to cooperate socially to the extent that they know how, but they are in need of constant guidance, guardianship, and friendship. The real effort that they are willing to put into social cooperation in the "shanty towns" where outcasts gather, if it could be brought to bear in a better environment, would be a potentially important resource for both these people themselves and for the total community.

Retarded persons develop real emotional attachments (Edgerton, 1967), and a retarded family often maintains a high level of friendship and affection sometimes a good deal higher than is found in marriages between normal people. If the remainder of the community can be brought to understand that retarded families are an expected part of the community and should have help and guidance, they can maintain a group of people whose contribution, if in no other way than through unskilled labor, can be very high.

Needs of the Retarded Family

Community support becomes even more important as children come into the retarded family. Such a family often can handle one or two children relatively well, both within their financial and their emotional resources, but as more children arrive the family tends to break down because the increased number of interpersonal contacts and the increased need for specialized decisions move beyond the capability of any of the members. Careful family planning and readily available information about contraceptives is highly necessary if such families are to be maintained without disaster. And the maintenance of them is certainly desirable from the point of view of society; they meet the socio-sexual needs of their members just as do marriages between normal people. If society does not see to the survival of retarded as families it automatically will be reinforcing a higher incidence of promiscuity and prostitution.

Thus we need to consider how such a family can be helped. Their primary need is for some sort of continuing education program which must include both parents and children. The continuing education should emphasize vocational training; as the family develops it will need higher income and so its wage earner should be given training that will make him eligible for advancement if the opportunity arises (Blackman & Siperstein, 1968; Fenton & Thompson, 1967). If their functioning is so limited that they are only capable of employment in a **contract workshop** or sheltered-environment situation, then additional opportunities should be worked out so that both husband and wife are employed but still able to give appropriate care to their children. The process of continuing education becomes one of social maintenance on the one hand and maintenance of their right to be contributing members of society on the other.

There also are more specific needs of family training. There may have to be, for example, an intensive quick course in budgeting, or in telling time, or in signing their names so that they can play a more normal role in community affairs. This sort of training should be drawn from the resources of community agencies most involved with the mentally retarded, and the training should be available even though the family is not a full-time client of the agency. Both members of the family should be trained to market, to cook, to do minor household repairs, and to do most of the other things that a normal individual learns before he leaves home. Training activities of this sort usually must be initiated by the agencies involved, for the retarded persons are not aware that they do not know.

Thus there is an extensive need for **outreach** contact into these families, to find out what areas of correction might be introduced through training programs. The people who make these contacts must be trained to determine what the retarded individuals do know as well as what they do not know, so that the outreach workers neither become overprotective and do too much, nor presume that this adult couple who to some degree are succeeding on their own are really just children playing house. It requires care and skill to see that the outreach function increases the clients' independence rather than reinforcing their dependence.

Where there are children, their role in family training becomes increasingly important. We have already noted that if young, potentially retarded children can be put into appropriate preschool programs, much can be done with them. If the community agencies assume their responsibility and improve the nutritional, disease prevention, and other health aspects of the living situation, and if the children are given the proper educational help at the preschool age, by the time they go to school there is a high probability that they can enter a regular class. We then have a situation in which the developing children are more able and proficient than their parents. The improved educational and emotional situation brought about through the development of the self-concept and cognitive abilities of the child then come together to make a healthier, more stable, more livable family unit. In this way the child himself can become part of the development of the parents, who will benefit immensely from the increased level of functioning which the child is able to demonstrate.

In Sum . . .

Thus we see that child-family-community interaction is crucial, and that it must continue from the first introduction of the retarded child to his family throughout his lifetime, including his old age. During the life span of a retarded person there are three key matters that must be emphasized. First, the problem of retardation must be identified early and the parents must be included early in the problem-solving process. Second, the family of a retarded person must be made a primary resource for his change and growth. Third, there must be lifelong planning for any person who has aspects of permanent dependency.

Retarded people should have the opportunity to live normal, contributing lives. They should maintain their own families if they are capable of doing so, and it is to the advantage of the community that they be encouraged in the effort and helped to sustain their marriages. We, as members of the community, must understand that these people are human beings just as we are and that they have as much right as we to an accepted place in the social structure. Parents should plan toward this end, and communities should help make it possible by a variety of services.

11

Development of Community Programs

Current mental retardation services do not meet community needs. Long-term custodial care, the least desirable service, is not being replaced by other types of residential programs or by programs to maintain handicapped people at home or in their local communities.

Programs should be organized upon the basic principle of providing as much service as possible to the family at the neighborhood level, gradually moving to larger geographic organizations only as neighborhood services prove inefficient. This approach will permit the mentally retarded to remain whenever possible, in their own homes; if that fails, to remain in their own communities; and only if that fails to be placed in state facilities. In this chapter we will propose certain programs that have accomplished these ends under more limited circumstances (Lent, LeBlanc, & Spradlin, 1967; Risley, 1968).

To achieve these desirable ends, a complete change in social attitudes toward retardation will be required—a change that must start with the neighborhood,[1] for it is essential that young children be helped as early in their lives as possible, and the neighborhood is where the youngest are found. Major influences on child development occur during the preschool period. These include sensory-motor development, differentiation of cognitive cues, adaptation to

[1] A neighborhood is defined as a catchment area of 25,000 to 30,000 people.

the immediate environment, initial learning of communication skills, origination of social competence, and initiation of various other abilities related to human growth and development (Yarrow, 1968).

Training Begins Early

The earlier a child can be seen by a competent professional, the more specific are the difficulties that can be handled. Even newborn infants who have various kinds of physical difficulties or evidence of sensory or cognitive malfunctions can be helped. Much of the child-development research in the area of orienting reflexes and early development of sensory and cognitive abilities shows evidence of early response patterns, although the exact nature of these abilities and the extent to which they develop during the period from birth to about two-and-a-half years of age is yet uncertain. We do know, however, that essential early learning, in terms of brain growth and development, occurs before the age of four. Thus preschool training should begin during the first four years. Specialized experience with nursery schools and group organizations has verified this point (Bessell, 1968). All children, regardless of where they may be on the learning curve, can benefit from such early preschool experiences (Kidd, 1968).

The youngest children—those under two or two-and-a-half years—cannot easily be taken from their homes and brought to clinics. Such a move would not only be inconvenient for a child and its parents, but might actually be dangerous to the baby who would thus be involved in numerous clinic contacts. Further, once the home patterns were disrupted in this way, all that could be studied would be the disruption effects. Therefore once the attending physician, hospital staff, or visiting nurse identifies the young child who has a problem, home trainers and outreach workers should be introduced into the family (Arnold & Goodman, 1966) to help them develop the corrective procedures required. Children who do not present problems may receive whatever additional help the parents request for accelerating their training. If there are concrete needs—such as those for nutritional or sanitation guidance—the home trainer or

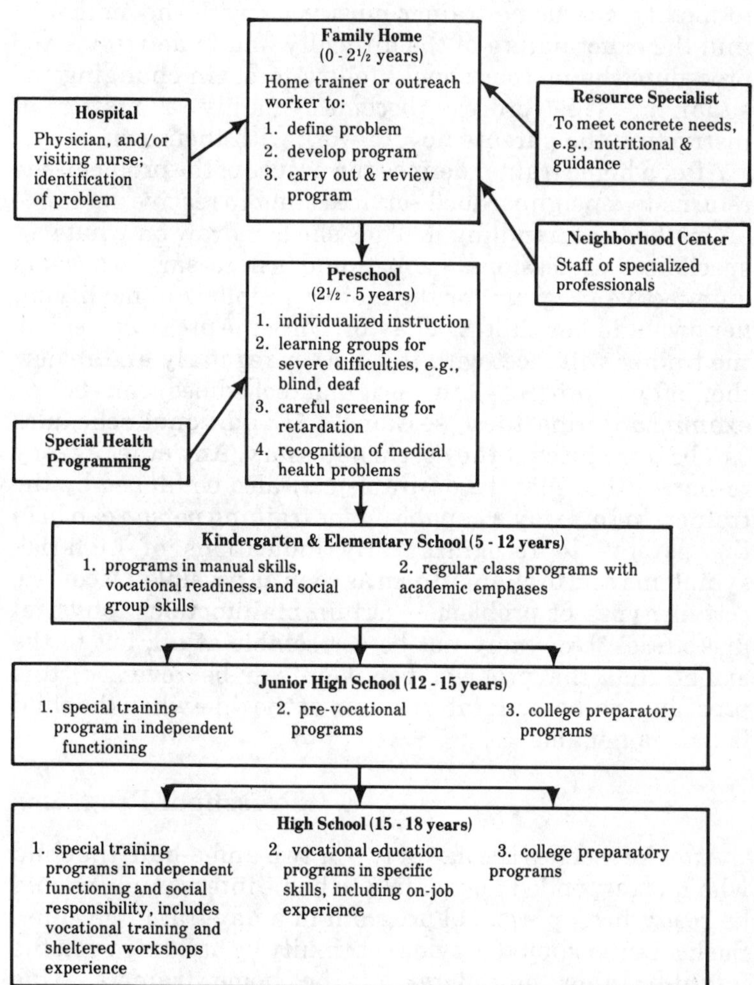

Figure 1. Resource Relationships for Growth and Maturation

outreach person can call in a resource specialist to help the parents make the necessary corrections. On the other hand, if there is a functional difficulty present that will require time to modify, the home trainer must work with the mother to find the exact nature of the difficulty and to determine the procedure the mother should follow to begin changing the situation. This process becomes mainly a matter of instructing the parents how to work with their own baby.

After a home trainer defines the nature of the problem, she returns to a neighborhood service center to receive guidance on methods of handling it. Thus she can draw on whatever specialized professional background is necessary to develop an effective program for the mother to follow in modifying her own and her child's behavior. Once the program begins, the trainer will meet with the mother regularly and review the baby's progress; the original schedules can be re-examined during these sessions and additional schedules can be introduced if they seem necessary. Any other agency resources that may be desirable can also be tapped by the trainer. In this way a capable home training person can help the parents to recognize early indications of high-risk symptoms and to change them as soon as possible. Of course, certain types of problems—certain malfunctions, physical disabilities, etc.—may not be correctable at all, but to the extent that the problem behavior can be reversed, this procedure will permit intervention at the time when the child is most amenable.

Preschool Programs

After he reaches the age of two or two-and-a-half, the child who has responded adequately to home intervention should be ready for a preschool program in a day-training center. Such a center should provide continuity by building upon the infant-training procedures of the home trainers. This approach has been used over the years by the Montessori schools[2] and other, similar, establishments. Preschool programs should not involve extensive diagnostic testing and establishment of psychological norms—norms that may

[2]An exposition of this type of approach may be had from Children's House, 2145 Central Parkway, Cincinnati, Ohio.

be hurtful to the program by limiting expectation and creating premature labeling. There will be ability groups in these schools, but they will occur in terms of how children learn colors, judge weights, understand length or roundness, etc. Each child should be able to work at his own speed, and the norms to be used should be group norms that make it possible for the extent of lag to be determined so that training priorities can be fixed (Smith, 1971, pp. 110-114).

Some children will no doubt learn heights and weights, for example, more quickly than others, but as these are specific, finite tasks, nearly all children can learn them eventually without any need for differential labeling. Vocational research with older mentally retarded people has demonstrated that while there is an obvious difference between the normal and the retarded person at the beginning of a specific task, the retarded person catches up as training increases, until eventually the levels of efficiency for both the retarded and normal are indistinguishable (Baumeister, 1967; 1968). There may be a different learning pace, but once the task has been learned, the performance does not reflect this difference in pace (Williams, 1970). Thus once a finite task is learned, the differential intelligence is no longer a problem with that task (Tsikoto, 1968). It is apparent that the only way the normal child maintains an advanced pace is by constantly receiving new learning tasks, and that all but the most severely retarded can be expected to learn in time the basic, straightforward processes necessary for everyday living.

Preschool training experience is particularly valuable in overcoming the effects of inadequate opportunity, because it is not tied to a fixed curriculum or a set schedule as is schooling for older children. Another aspect of learning at this "basic skills" level is the need to add new material constantly to the child's work without first waiting for him to complete previous units (Smith, D., 1959; Smith, R., 1971). If the child finds a particular learning task extremely difficult, the program must be able to provide other tasks at which he will be more adept. The cognitive development that will occur as the result of success in the other areas will raise the entire learning curve (Young, 1969). In this way, if the child does not present severe learning difficulties or distinct biomedical abberations by the time he is ready to go into kindergarten, he will be on a par with his unimpaired peers and can proceed with them. If he does present more intense problems, he will still be better able to benefit from later specialized training.

During the preschool years a variety of medically-related difficulties may emerge. Some children will demonstrate convulsive behavior, some will show various kinds of orthopedic handicaps, and some will be found to have internal malformations such as defects of the heart (sometimes due to rheumatic fever) or other organs. If these children are brought together into a public program it will be easier to apply medical services earlier, and special health programming can be set up around groups of children who have similar defects—groups such as **cardiac** problems, the blind, the deaf, and the orthopedically handicapped.

Children with marginal medical difficulties often are not identified until they come to school. Those who have trouble seeing may not acquire glasses until quite late, or those with hearing impairment may not receive help soon enough. Such problems would be recognized earlier in a group preschool situation, and corrective action could be started at a much earlier age than is now common. Physicians working with children of this sort would also learn more about child development and learning processes.

During the preschool period, those who present severe learning difficulties can be identified and separated into groups that will be provided special kinds of help. One can visualize a physical-therapy-oriented-stair-climbing group, a how-you -hold-a-spoon group, or how-you-transfer - liquid-from-one-cup-to-another group. At a higher level there could be a removing-coat group, a cooperating-with-peers group, or a making-oral-requests group. If the severely impaired child enters school during the preschool period, the division from academic emphasis will begin when it should (Scheerenberger, 1971), and he will be given the training he needs at the earliest possible time.

In this way the youngster who today is described as an EMR child (educable mentally retarded, requiring special education) would have his difficulties modified during the preschool training period and would no longer require separation from his peers, although he might still require special approaches (Fitzsimmons, Cheever, Leonard, & Macunovich, 1969). He might still be a **slow learner** (Smith, 1967) or because of continued sociocultural deprivation be faced with social differences that make it difficult for him to maintain himself in a regular curriculum (Erdman & Olson, 1966), but there would be no need for separate EMR classes.

The special approaches to such children should be based neither on the label of mental retardation nor on the present concept of special education, but instead should deal with specific aspects of learning and adaptive behavior—aspects that can also be dealt with in leisure-time activities and other areas of social interaction (Goodman, 1969). As an example, children from poverty areas often come to school with a special language; during the formative years they learned what can be called the dialect of their specific social region (Baratz and Shuy, 1969; Shuy, 1969). Such children should not be described as mentally retarded and put through a special education curriculum, but rather should be taught English as though it were a foreign language. There are similar examples in all of the academic areas where children who at first appear to have deficiencies are not really deficient, but merely different. Their differences must be considered in their curricula so that they learn to communicate and deal with the dominant culture, but they should not be labeled as retarded for they can only be harmed by that label.

Other groups present a more consistent pattern of learning difficulty. Mild forms of such difficulties can be alleviated during the preschool period. Even with help, however, this group is not attuned to high levels of academic training (though some individuals within it may be), and the emphasis here should be that most will function in manual work rather than becoming brain workers (Conant, 1961). It is difficult to predict exactly what manual skills will be needed when these children graduate, because technological changes occur so rapidly in our environment, but we can presume that there still will be a vast number of personal services and similar areas which will require hand skills. The slower children should be placed in a curriculum that leads them to this sort of career, so that their success experiences can exceed their failure experiences.

All of this is not to say that there are no truly retarded children. Obviously there are many. With them, preschool training would provide valuable screening, for during it and before they entered regular school they would clearly identify themselves as belonging to a completely different category, and their special difficulties could then be approached in a separate program. They need special buildings, designed in a special way, with special facilities. For example, if a child is not yet toilet-trained, it becomes the responsibility of the school to train him. Toilet training, like any other learning process, is a matter of imitation and demonstrative understanding. If we have a class of ten children who need toilet training, we need a schoolroom that has ten stools so that the ten children can be part of a toilet-training exercise following each other's cues. The process would not fit the atmosphere of the typical classroom. Similar processes are related to other personal hygiene procedures, to feeding procedures, to dressing procedures, etc., and a different kind of space with special facilities is required for each of them (Watson, 1964).

Emphasis on academics for a child at this level is a waste of time. We are more concerned with his time than with his teacher's—she is being paid, but the child has only a limited span within which to learn things that will be valuable to him and that will let him enter sheltered employment, contract workshops, or other vocational endeavors (Jacobs & Weingold, 1958; Cohen, 1961). He must not lose time by trying to learn material which he will neither use nor make a part of his life. Emphasis should be placed on sensory-motor and related personality and attitudinal requirements for his becoming a contributing member of society. Since children at this level demonstrate a variety of training deficiencies, the teacher must be free to establish priorities. These priorities should be based on both the critical demands of the community and on current behaviors. Since successes are more rewarding than failures the priorities for training should be based on available skills ("hills") rather than on those absent ("valleys").

Schooling

Through kindergarten and elementary school we should have separate curricula with separate facilities, one designed for a variety of manual skill programs intended to develop vocational readiness and for development of the group skills that children need in order to live and work together, the other presenting regular classes that have academic emphasis. Children are selected for these programs on the basis of their preschool histories. Those who go into special classes are the ones who, after three years of preschool experience, still have major deficiencies in the area of independent functioning and self-help skills. These special learning classes will be designed to improve skills and to build up each child's motivation and self-concept to a point where he can achieve a better learning set, again with emphasis on the "hill" and "valley" approach. Generally, these classes will deal with the needs of children who probably will never be able to move into direct academic situations. But, at the junior-high-school level the two groups must be brought together for reassessment and redistribution into three general areas. The first area would be college preparatory, for students who could be expected to go into further academic and professional training. The second area would be pre-vocational, for children who would prepare for a trade or other non-academic occupation. The third area would be for those children who have to remain in a training program for the mentally retarded and handicapped youngsters who have not yet accomplished their training objectives.

It should not be assumed automatically that the child who has been in a class for the trainable mentally retarded throughout his elementary years would continue in such a class through junior high school, or that the child who has been in a regular class would necessarily continue in it. A definite reassessment should be made of each individual, and each should be placed in the appropriate curriculum. The prevocational classes and the special classes might overlap in the sense that both groups of students need similar kinds of training in terms of fine motor skills, job expectations, knowledge of tools, and so on; but in other instances the classes would be distinctly separate, with the special classes putting emphasis on continuation of the teaching of independent functioning and skill subjects such as budgeting, telling time, writing, and spelling. Thus, where both levels of student can work and learn together, the school should make it possible for them to do so and only require separation when it is really necessary. This program should continue for the three years of junior high and then once again the students should be brought together for further assessment and for high-school programming.

The high school program should also be divided into the three types of classes. The college-preparatory classes should emphasize those subjects necessary for college entrance. The pre-vocational classes should, at this level, become vocational education classes where specific skills and training would be provided to ready the students for employment upon graduation; they should be coupled with work-opportunity situations, so that students in this program would spend part of each day in school, learning skills and allied academic subjects, and part on the job. The special-training program in the high school should also be oriented in this manner, so that the student spends part of each day in school, continuing to gain further development of specific areas of independent functioning, and the other part of the day in vocational-rehabilitation-sponsored training programs or sheltered employment where he could improve his actual working skills and learn to be employable (*Mental Retardation Abstracts,* 1965).

All students should enter high school and all students should receive the same kind of graduation diploma. Differences in training should not be marked on diplomas. The transcripts of those in college training would show that they had the necessary background, and certificates of excellence in certain training areas or of apprenticeship qualification should be given members of the other two groups. In this way all will have evidence of high-school graduation, something they will need for a number of purposes in the future.

This plan provides a way of dealing with the educational needs of normal, developmentally disabled, and retarded people from birth through entrance into vocational areas. Throughout this plan the groups which are organized are not blocs, and when the needs are met a specific group is dissolved and the individuals move on to other groups at the next developmental level; further, a child in a color-recognition group would not necessarily be in the same group for tying, since he might learn the two activities at different paces. However, all have the same set of objectives which include normalization of self-help skills, improved independent functioning, broadening activities of daily living, and maturation of personal and social responsibility.

This plan does not completely do away with labeling, but it uses the label only with those children who have clear-cut learning deficiencies which cannot be reversed through systematic programs. Children with educational retardation or the type of learning deficiencies which can be modified through special approaches in a regular classroom do not need the label "retarded" and will learn better and more fully if they do not have it.

Such an approach should also lead to different ways of handling regular classes. Work with the mentally retarded in EMR classes has developed procedures that could be used equally well in regular classes (McCarthy & Scheerenberger, 1966; Watson, 1964). In fact, the regular-class student has in one sense been a disadvantaged student, for the best and most efficient means of training have not been used in his program, especially at the elementary-school level. The knowledge gained through experimentation related to EMR should be used to help all children, superior through slow learner. Individual types of curriculum planning, special one-to-one organization of daily programming, attention of teacher aides at times of special need, use of training machines and other teaching supports, sense training, imitation, specialization of learning processes, and interlocking core activities, all of which are the most advanced special education processes, should also be put to use in regular classes.

There are retarded people who, in addition to their primary retardation, also demonstrate emotional disturbance, physical disability, family disruptions, and major disruptions in life-support areas such as malnutrition and poor disease control. These people need services that will help them with all of their problems—services, however, that do not necessarily take them out of the school-vocational pattern. Thus the second major aspect of community programming becomes service delivery.

Community Services

Delivery of services is usually represented in terms of community, state, and national responsibilities. Here, too, primary emphasis should be placed upon the community or neighborhood, and the area of concern should be broadened only as necessary to provide services that the neighborhood cannot offer (Leland, 1973b). Here, too, as in the early stages of training, the major change agent should be the family of the retarded person. The family is at present one of the greatest untapped resources for the maintenance of retarded children. The family should be the group most responsible for such children, and they can be if they are provided the necessary supervision and appropriate allotments to help defray the costs of maintaining handicapped people at home.

We have seen that it is undesirable—even dangerous—to take small children to clinics except for real emergencies. Even with older children, the concept that services can be provided only by bringing them to a clinic not only forces an artificial approach to the problem, but also is demeaning to those we try to help. There are further difficulties if the clinics are operated by white professionals in areas where the major clientele represent minority groups. Even subtle approaches that lead them to the clinics will, in the long run, tend to be antitherapeutic. If the same clinic group will begin to develop talent indigenous to the area, and have this talent work with those who are in trouble so that there is already a built-in area of support and understanding, it will be much more effective. And the most efficient group of people who may be trained in this way are the parents of the children themselves.

Many of the families in the slum areas are on Aid to Dependent Children (ADC) and already represent a public

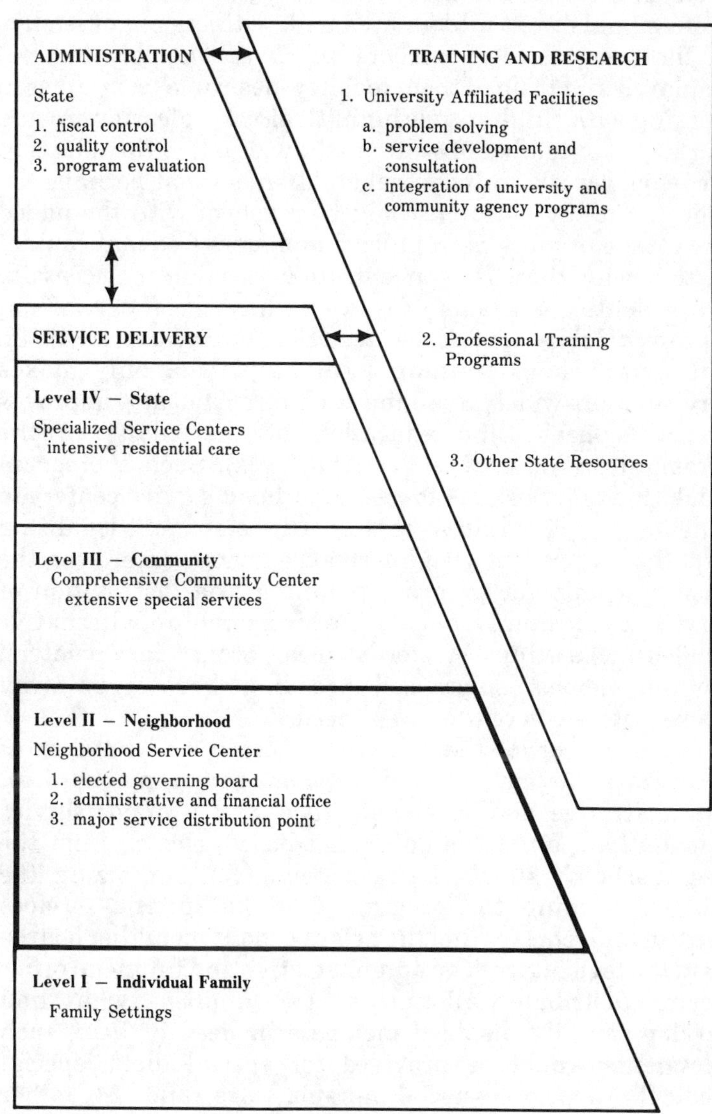

Figure 2. Community Service Development

trust. The same money now being spent on the dole could be used for salaries for them to work with their children. If professionals went into an area and, with the aid of leaders in the area, selected parents who were capable but not employed and trained them to follow desirable techniques in working with children, one highly trained professional could work with a number of willing adults. Each of the adults in turn could work with several children, so that perhaps ten times as many children could be reached, with the added advantage of more personalized and more frequent contact in this way than by concentration in clinics. Successful experimental programs of this sort have been carried out (Smith & Hobbs, 1966; *Spearhead at Juniper Gardens,* 1968). The approach of training local people not only makes services more widely available to children, but also improves the self-concept and education of the adults in the community (Wolfe, Giles, & Hall, 1968). Such a program would make it possible for neighborhood service centers to function as consultative centers. One also can visualize a situation where the neighborhood service center was the basis not only for program planning and distribution of services to the family, but also for sponsorship of alternative residential settings—foster homes, group care centers, nursing homes, supervised boarding houses, half-way houses, etc.—where they were needed.

The neighborhood service center could well have three organizational features: an indigenous governing board, an administrative and financial office, and a major service distribution point. The governing board, elected from the neighborhood, should be responsible for organizing the center, planning the program and the specific services needed, and representing the neighborhood on higher boards up to the legislature. The administrative and financial office would distribute allotments to families who had developmentally disabled members in need of help; such allotments would be provided for special diets, special medical attention, special nursing care, and any other special requirements necessary to maintain retarded individuals in their own homes. The major service distribution point, on the one hand, would be the home base for outreach personnel, home training personnel, visiting nurses, home management consultants, and others who would go out into the neighborhood homes to help families work with handicapped children; and on the other hand, it would provide a central location to which families could come for consultation, medical or other professional information, and assistance. Where specific services are not available in the center it would be able to purchase them on a contract basis (both within and outside the neighborhood). Thus a center of this kind could serve as the major point of reference for any handicapped person.

Such a center would have to come under the scrutiny of the state in the areas of fiscal control, standard setting and quality control, and program evaluation. One can envision an organization structure that would provide for local control of program priorities, hiring, and distribution of services, with state supervision of the application and maintenance of standards and monetary responsibility. The neighborhood centers should be free to initiate programs but the evaluative responsibility of the state should be developed as a regular and continuing process.

Because some children cannot remain in their own homes, and because as children become adults they will lose their parents, other residential facilities will be needed (these are described in more detail in the next chapter). Such residential facilities should not be mandatory, but any retarded person who functions within the scope of a particular facility should have it available. If a retarded person does not need protective services or a supervised environment, the neighborhood service center should help him either to maintain his own residence or to live in a regular boarding house within the neighborhood. It should provide advice on the problems of daily living and leisure time—problems ranging from employment through time purchases to marriage.

A vast amount of federal money is being expended (Roth, 1968) on research and demonstration programs. It is the responsibility of those doing the research to make sure that the information from the programs filters down to the people who are in close contact with service delivery, and it is the responsibility of clinical professionals to bring the information into the problem-solving area and make use of it. As pediatric medicine, child psychology, and child social work are expanded because of the increase in preschool programming, one would expect that professional training programs would also expand to include more and more of the child-development information derived from research efforts.

There will be some people, however, who because of the nature of their handicaps cannot be helped directly through their families or through their neighborhood service centers, but who must be given more sophisticated professional help from larger units with greater resources. Neighborhood service centers should make it possible for these people to visit comprehensive community centers[3] without having to drop out of school or leave their jobs. This could be done readily, for the community service centers would be based on groups of neighborhoods and would provide services in much the same general geographic areas as those neighborhoods. Further, the neighborhood centers should receive bloc grants from the states to enable them to pay for additional needed care and to help such people with a minimum of dislocation and economic pressure.

We have already discussed the fact that the concept of a separate comprehensive center for the retarded and another for the emotionally disturbed is both a taxpayers' disaster, because of unnecessary duplication of expenditures, and a professional disaster, because of emphasis on differential diagnosis. A child who constantly disrupts the classroom because of a learning disability follows a pattern not too different from a child who constantly disrupts it because of emotional disturbance. Both children may be rude to the teacher, run around screaming, throw things, or hit other children; and both could benefit from similar types of play therapy (Leland & Smith, 1965). It is the disruptive activity that needs correcting, not the etiology of the learning problem. Clinicians have also found that if such behavioral maladaptions can be adjusted, other aspects of learning will go forward at a more rapid pace. Thus the goal is to relieve the problem so that training can progress. This is a typical

[3]A community comprehensive service center should represent a catchment area of approximately 150,000-200,000 people.

pattern followed when dealing with children in child guidance clinics, but the retarded have usually been excluded from it.

Comprehensive centers, in order to fulfill their extreme importance in the overall continuum of service, should provide for all areas of need (Klebanoff, 1964). Children who, for example, need special help in speech and hearing, psychotherapy, specific medical supervision in the use of psycho-pharmacological agents or seizure control, or help from the various activity therapies, should all have these services available to them at the comprehensive center without being excluded from school and without being provided "hotel service" by the state. They should live at home, where the parents should be part of the therapeutic process, and they should remain in their usual classrooms unless they are disrupting them; if they are disrupting, they should be removed only long enough for the psychotherapy to work and then should be returned.

In addition to considering these programs in terms of the services to be provided, we might also consider the kinds of people who will receive the services. Most of the retarded who fall typically into adaptive levels I and II (Leland, Nihira, Foster, Shellhaas, & Kagin, 1968) should be provided for by the changes in the educational system. They will be in a school system where they will receive the training they need except for possible disorders requiring special intervention. But lower functional people may not be as easily provided the necessary services. Those at the lowest levels probably will need intensive day care (Conover, 1971) and other specialized services including, in some instances, residential facilities. Those in intermediate adaptive categories make up a mixed group, some of whom have biomedical deficiencies that need more extensive intervention and some of whom have behavior disorders that need more extensive supervision. In either instance, the comprehensive center should provide the necessary resources.

It is difficult to forecast what effect the neighborhood centers and the comprehensive community centers would have on other services. If more and more children can be helped at the local level, however, a smaller number of children will later need intensive help. The available specialized professionals should then be able to do a better job, for their total caseloads would be smaller.

An approach through neighborhood and community centers is not particularly new. In fact, it is inherent in the whole concept of public health services. Public health services have been applied primarily to the medical needs of the community and to problems relating to sanitation, disease control, and epidemiology. The same approach can be used effectively in the mental health area, and both the prevention of mental retardation and mental illness and the control of all mental disorders can be seen in the same context as public health problems.[4]

Some people have disorders and problems that cannot be met through any available services because of a current lack of professional knowledge. If the information from research and experience that is now available in the area of mental retardation and associated disorders could be fully applied, we would be able to deal with many more problems through community facilities (Secretary's Committee on Mental Retardation, 1968). But there will still remain a number of people afflicted by disorders and mental aberrations which have not yet responded to research or clinical procedures. They need specialized programs and, as a last resort, state residential care. No child should be included in a specialized institution unless there is no other resource available or unless we have no other idea of what to do with him.

University-Affiliated Facilities

As the result of Public Law 88-164, passed in 1963, a number of centers have been developed in affiliation with the major universities of the country. They were established to give professional training on an interdisciplinary basis and to provide an innovative service of direct intervention programs in the treatment needs of retarded individuals.

[4]The National Institute of Mental Health has published a series of specific pamphlets that describe the major services of a community mental health center. Most of this information also applies directly to mental retardation centers (National Institute of Mental Health, 1969).

They fill in between the comprehensive community service centers and the specialized residential institutions.

To perform their training function, these **university-affiliated facilities** are staffed primarily by professors and their students. In this way specialists are developed in the field of mental retardation who at the same time receive the general training required by their own disciplines. The centers provide interdisciplinary training in a multi-discipline program; the people who graduate from the program are specialists in the areas of developmental disabilities, mental retardation, and allied handicaps. Patients in these facilities are those for whose problems there are no ready answers. The centers provide a direct problem-solving service for them, while at the same time evolving new ways of delivering services, conceiving and testing programs, and integrating university programs with community-agency programs. Because of the type of patients, the activities of the facility are tied directly to research. Everything done with the patients is exploratory and is aimed toward solving their problems—and thus toward solving the problems of whole categories of people who are similarly afflicted. The centers bring together under one roof the major elements of a training, service, and research program with a problem-solving orientation. They provide most of what previously has been done by the better state residential institutions without having also to provide extensive residential services.

Usually these university-affiliated programs also have the statewide responsibilities of providing consultants for agencies throughout the state and for making the retardation services of the university available to citizens anywhere in the state. In addition, they reach out into other states to cooperate with similar centers elsewhere. This cooperation opens the possibility of developing regional and eventually national data banks and experience groups which would permit demonstrations requiring a greater population than might be available to a single center, and which would also permit the gathering of information that would then become available to centers and programs throughout the community. There is also the possibility of exchanging students and professors between facilities, so that the experience of one can be shared by others.

Beyond the people who can be helped at the university facilities there remains a small group with problems that can be helped only on an intensive, round-the-clock-basis. Highly specialized, centralized state institutions should be maintained for them.

Throughout the distribution of community services the problem is that of knowing who needs treatment, what type of treatment is needed, and where it should most appropriately occur. In identifying needs, we must select those people who most benefit from the label of "mentally retarded" and must then determine the kinds of service which would most benefit them. The greatest need at present is a modification of community attitudes which will permit the evolution of new kinds of service more appropriate to the needs of the retarded in the community. In any research, the most important thing is finding the right question to ask. In dealing with mental retardation as a community problem, the time has come to stop asking the question, "Where can the child be placed?" We now must ask, "What can be done to change specific behaviors that are most annoying to the community?" With this new question, a whole new field of services and clinical approaches becomes available.

12

Human Rights and Retarded People

Instead of asking how the retarded person differs from the normal, we should ask how he can be helped to meet essential community standards. He must be made relatively invisible—he must be helped to talk, walk, and dress like other people and, to the extent of his ability, react like them to a variety of situations. Above all, he must have the opportunity and right to live like other people. This is the process that has been described as "normalization" (Nirje, 1969)[1]; this concept embodies the major changes needed in the public attitude toward retardation.

An example of the difficulty in changing attitudes arises from the extreme visibility of some of the less common forms of retardation. This is largely a new phenomenon; historically most people with extreme forms of retardation did not live. But improved medical science has enabled them to survive in greater numbers, the general public has come into increasing contact with them, and its reaction has been a combination of pity and terror which has increased the demands for separation. Although such extreme retardation creates great difficulty in coping, they can be helped to gain greater social competence; but institutional separation often

[1]This concept may be easily misunderstood; there is no implication that retarded children can become "normal." Rather, it emphasizes that all individuals have the right to be treated and approached as normally as possible (Nirje, 1969; Wolfensberger, 1969).

negates the process (Mitchell & Smeriglio, 1970). Thus, even at this level, the normalization approach would be beneficial. All retarded persons, regardless of their level of handicap, can be helped. It is their right as human beings to receive this help.

In accordance with this philosophy, the process of normalization is based on the *Declaration of General and Special Rights of the Mentally Retarded* (1969), established by the International League of Societies for the Mentally Handicapped meeting in Stockholm, Sweden, on October 24, 1968. The declaration reads:

> Whereas *the universal declaration of human rights adopted by the United Nations proclaims that all of the human family without distinction of any kind, have equal and inalienable rights of human dignity and freedom:*
>
> Whereas *the declaration of the rights of the child, adopted by the United Nations, proclaims the rights of the physically, mentally or socially handicapped child to special treatment, education, and care required by his particular condition.*
>
> Now Therefore, the International League of Societies for the Mentally Handicapped expresses the general and special rights of the mentally retarded as follows:
>
> Article I: The mentally retarded person has the same basic rights as other citizens of the same country and same age.
>
> Article II: The mentally retarded person has a right to proper medical care and physical restoration and to such education, training, habilitation and guidance as will enable him to develop his ability and potential to the fullest possible extent, no matter how severe his degree of disability. No mentally handicapped person should be deprived of such services by reason of the costs involved.
>
> Article III: The mentally retarded person has a right to economic security and to a decent standard of living. He has a right to productive work or to other meaningful occupation.

Article IV: The mentally retarded person has a right to live with his own family or with foster parents; to participate in all aspects of community life, and to be provided with appropriate leisure time activities. If care in an institution becomes necessary it should be in surroundings and under circumstances as close to normal living as possible.

Artivle V: The mentally retarded person has a right to a qualified guardian when this is required to protect his personal well-being and interests. No person rendering direct services to the mentally retarded should also serve as his guardian.

Article VI: The mentally retarded person has a right to protection from exploitation, abuse and degrading treatment. If accused, he has a right to a fair trial and full recognition being given to his degree of responsibility.

Article VII: Some mentally retarded persons may be unable, due to the severity of their handicap, to exercise for themselves all of these rights in a meaningful way. For others, modification of some or all of the rights is appropriate. The procedure used for modification or denial of rights must contain proper legal safeguards against every form of abuse, must be based on an evaluation of the social capability of the mentally retarded persons by qualified experts and must be subject to periodic reviews and to the right of appeal to higher authorities.

ABOVE ALL—THE MENTALLY RETARDED PERSON HAS THE RIGHT TO RESPECT.

Some retarded people cannot always exercise these human rights to the fullest. The level of their retardation, the nature of their disability, and the needs of the family and the community all intervene from time to time. But we always must approach the problem in such a way as to insure that every individual receives the specific help he needs, and the opportunity to develop further. His need for help must be defined by evaluations that determine what he can or cannot do for himself (Leland, 1973a) and then be considered together with special community conditions—for example, is it an urban or rural, industrial or residential community?—to arrive at what specific facilities should be provided by this community to this person (Edgerton, 1967). In the past the question was approached with a "well-let's-build-something" attitude in a sincere effort to meet observable needs (Warner, Queen, & Harper, 1942), following the principle that hungry people should be fed or sick people treated. These people could not function in their environment, so they were placed in institutions where they could function. The major error was not the building of institutions or even the placing of the retarded in them, but rather a public assumption that the needs of the retarded include protection, both for themselves and for the community, and that this protection could best be furnished by separation (Deutsch, 1952).

A different, more appropriate approach will have to be based on a public attitude leading toward normalization. The first major change must be based on the right of the retarded to remain in their home community. The idea of having retarded people in the community has become more acceptable to the public, but so far there is little general understanding of what facilities should be available for them.

A community-based "life planning" program for all levels of disability should provide for the broadening of options and the guarantee of human rights. This life planning program should include vocational and personal independence training and housing.

Day-Training Centers

The retarded person who needs to make the greatest number of adaptations also needs the earliest possible help. Thus for the severely and profoundly retarded infant, a family-based program should start as soon as feasible. As the children develop, day-training centers become the most essential part of public programming (Conover, 1971; Murphy & Scheerenberger, 1971). Children who cannot be helped in the school system but who are able to remain at home as a result of **family allotments,** visiting nurses, home trainers, and similar help, also need centers where they

TRAINING FOR VOCATIONAL AND PERSONAL INDEPENDENCE

AGE GROUP / Functional Level	Independent	Semi-independent	Dependent
Infant	day training center	day training center	day training center or home trainer
Child	school	pre-vocational training in school	self-help and social group skills in special schools
Adolescent	vocational center	vocational training in school	pre-vocational training in special schools
Adult	regular employment	sheltered employment or sheltered contract workshop	independent functioning training and sheltered workshop

HOUSING

AGE GROUP / Functional Level	Independent	Semi-independent	Dependent
Infant	family's home or foster home	family's home or group care home	family's home or nursing home
Child	family's home or foster home	family's home, foster home, or group care home	family's home, nursing home, or specialized institution
Adolescent	family's home or boarding home	family's home, group care home, or half-way house	family's home, nursing home, or specialized institution
Adult	own home or boarding home	boarding home or half-way house	family's home, nursing home, or specialized institution
Elderly	own home, family's home, or geriatric center	family's home or geriatric center	nursing center

Figure 3. Life Planning for the Developmentally Disabled

can receive specific training and guidance in coping with their handicaps so that they will not be too visible. For these children day-training centers take the place of schools and provide intensive training and treatment, thus not only promoting the growth and development of the severely retarded youngsters but also making it possible to keep them at home by relieving their parents of the stress of caring for them around the clock.

Therefore the first major-care facilities we must consider are appropriate day-training centers distributed geographically through the population areas. Children of school age unable to participate in those classes for the trainable mentally retarded that usually are offered by the school systems could be brought in to these centers. As the children develop, some might be transferred to other classes and others might stay with the day-training program through pre-vocational and vocational training. These facilities must be developed to provide for the part of the school-age retarded population that would otherwise have to be institutionalized (Murphy & Scheerenberger, 1971).

Services for Older Retarded Persons

Older retarded persons also have special needs (Katz, 1968). At the point where they leave school we must be concerned with their right to become contributing members of society. To accomplish this we need two sets of objectives, one for those who can enter into the industrial structure and another for those who will always need some type of sheltered employment.

The former need to go from school into special vocational centers designed to train retarded young adults in specific activities. Here they should be trained to do jobs needed by the community and also trained in daily living activities, including the use of leisure time and the development of life plans in relationship to their jobs. They should also receive specific counseling for job placement and eventual absorption into the community (Heber, 1963).

A life schedule intended to fit a retarded person into the community literally has to be charted. It must include a time for shopping, a time for taking care of laundry, a time for paying bills, a time for housecleaning, a time for personal hygiene, a time for just having fun, and so on. The person has to learn that he must maintain this **time budget** on an obligatory, routine basis, and that the myriad activities his life requires have to be done at identical times on identical days each week. It is impossible to build all potential activities into such a life schedule, and so events will develop that produce major deviations from the set schedule. The individual must be taught that when this happens he should consult immediately with his vocational counselor, if only briefly by telephone. The master time budget, like a master financial budget, should be reviewed periodically by the counselor to insure that it still is realistic for the individual. A system of this sort is essential; the obligatory routine minimizes social confusion and conserves the person's cognitive potential for the great number of unpredictable, everyday coping decisions he must face (Dingman, 1968).

The retarded who are unable to follow a program for independent living need a different set of vocational objectives. These should be reflected in facilities that provide sheltered living and sheltered employment (Speijer, 1968), the latter provided by contract workshops for which the community assumes full responsibility. These workshops should not necessarily be self-supporting, but should be considered essential community facilities just as schools are essential community facilities. There are many constructive forms of sheltered employment, and we must get away from the older idea that it consists only of a makeshift assembly line in the middle of a cement floor and that it produces only clay pots or wooden trellises. Landscape contracting could be undertaken, for instance, with the individuals being responsible for maintenance of parks and playgrounds; or sanitation contracting, with the handicapped acting as adjunct workers to the regular sanitation department crew. Such retarded workers could carry out a whole range of ecological activities as well; they could collect glass and paper, operate recycling equipment, clear out dumps, fill holes, and do many similar jobs.

Housing Facilities

Residential units for the retarded must be placed throughout the community. The primary unit, especially for a child, should be the home; there the retarded child should also be supported by the various community services we have discussed. When, under stress of particular conditions, the child must be placed elsewhere, either for his own good or for that of his family, the community must provide the necessary living arrangements (Wolfensberger, 1969; Appell & Tisdall, 1968).

Some retarded persons, both children and adults, would need to be housed in **total care units,** where twenty-four hour nursing and medical care are available. This does not mean that the person would spend all twenty-four hours in bed, however. To the extent practicable, various types of treatment and rehabilitation must be provided, even if they are nothing more than transferring the patient from his cot to the floor so that he can roll around with more freedom. A person who can be taught to turn himself over in bed or to open his mouth and swallow when being fed will be a more comfortable person and an easier one to care for. Such a housing unit should have a caring, happy atmosphere. A unit for these profoundly retarded people would have five or six beds at most, and should have the appropriate nursing staff in attendance with medical personnel available on call.

Going up the functional scale of the residents, the next type of living unit would be the sheltered environment, which we have already mentioned. Here there is a high degree of freedom of movement, but it is coupled with necessary supervision and guidance. The people who live here would differ from those in total-care units by being able to function and make decisions when giving additional support. For young children, group homes with up to ten individuals each seem desirable, either on farms in rural areas or in some of the large houses found in urban areas; here the children could be nurtured and loved in an atmosphere of community living and cooperation. These children would go to school somewhere outside the group home. They would have responsibilities in the home and the home would have the responsibility to provide them with as high a degree of freedom as they can tolerate, but mainly their joint purpose would be learning, through interaction, imitation; and support, how to function in the community on a more normal and less visible basis. In addition to the necessary medical, psychological, and social support for such a residence, there must be in charge of it house parents who provide a stable, loving environment.

Similar facilities should be available for adolescents and adults, particularly those given sheltered employment. These facilities might be called "retarded boarding houses." This is not to say that such a place would become an institution away from the institution, but rather that it would be a center of cooperative help and guidance in a small setting where everyone involved has some understanding of what is to be accomplished. Everyone in them would be carrying out a community function, such as going to school or working, and the aim would be to develop as homelike an atmosphere as possible through the inter-cooperation of those involved. The houses should also offer some guidance and supervision of both leisure time and daily living activities.

Retarded people at this level do need special follow-up contact because they have a continuing pattern of dependency. Guidance personnel could then provide supervision and help as needed. The building itself should be a normal residence of the community in which it is located and should not be marked or specially identified in any way.

These boarding houses would be supervised by what we call the "foster landlady"—a person who would have some training and who would be under contract to the neighborhood service center or other body providing part of the support for the house. She would be expected to intervene in any critical situation requiring careful judgment. Such situations would include signing of time payment contracts, switching jobs, or changing residences. Otherwise she would not interfere or control, but would always be available as a resource for the boarders.

In this same category there should be a third type of sheltered living for elderly retarded people whose level of dependency due to **senescence** is increasing rather than declining. They should be kept as independent as possible as long as possible, but since they are declining rapidly because of a combination of retardation, physical disability, and encroaching senility, a different life plan must be evolved for them (Talkington & Chiovaro, 1969). Thus these **geriatric centers** would need a greater number of additional-care personnel, who must encourage their patients to maintain a secure self-concept and as much independence as possible.

The highest children on the functional scale, those who for some reason cannot remain in their own homes but whose abilities and potential for independence are high enough that they do not belong in a sheltered-care unit, must be placed in foster homes. The community must accept the responsibility for maintaining foster homes in which one or two children could live in a home-like setting with some degree of continuity and security. In the past one of the greatest crimes of the foster-home system, as the result of poor planning or insufficient funding, has been the placing of a child in three or four different homes in the course of a year. Such constant movement creates many problems for the children and makes their rehabilitation exceptionally difficult (Douglas & Bloomfield, 1958). The community has a responsibility to insure that continuity is provided and maintained in a home-like atmosphere for these children.

Foster homes for retarded adults should emphasize independent living to the fullest extent possible. This means that the house parents must be available to give advice on all the normal daily activities which require careful decision-making, but that they must not interfere with the independence of the adult as long as he maintains himself, stays on his job or with his vocational counselor, and functions appropriately. The adult should be encouraged to contribute as much as possible to the maintenance of the home where he lives; there is nothing more dehumanizing than to put a person into a situation where he has no responsibility for his own maintenance and well-being. If he is totally provided for by other people he degenerates and becomes non-functional; such procedures, though they may sound "kind," only violate the human potential. Whenever possible, he should be encouraged to establish his own home.

Thus there is a wide variety of settings to which many of those who now are in institutions could profitably be transferred. Those patients who can be productive and can care for themselves should be released to sheltered community settings or half-way houses where they can become useful citizens. Those who can care for themselves but who cannot yet do productive work should be transferred to residential units or group homes where they can live in some freedom among those of like age and ability. Those who have problems in caring for themselves should be sent when possible to their families, but otherwise to nursing homes where they would receive the same level of care now provided in the best institutions. Only those who present serious management problems might have to remain in institutions, but these establishments should be designed especially to handle specific kinds of problems. In general, the existing programs should be modified to prevent the premature senility and the rapid rate of deterioration currently found in institutions (Bair & Leland, 1959; O'Connor, Justice, & Warren, 1970).

The statistics now available are not complete, but it seems clear that the smallest number of retarded are those who are most profoundly retarded. As we go up the scale there are many more people who need less care and could to some degree be self-supporting. Thus it is possible that the establishment of the facilities we have outlined and the phasing out of large general-purpose institutions would considerably reduce the total cost of caring for retarded people.

There are many people who for many reasons must be kept for short periods in rigid structures with tight controls. Therefore some type of institutional program would have to be maintained. This program should not, however, be based on the traditional concept of lifetime commitment. Instead, the individual should go into the institution; receive training, treatment, and whatever other procedures are required to meet his needs; and should then be returned to the community and take his place in one of the settings we have just described, either in a community facility, his own home, or a completely independent situation, according to the success of the institution program (Woloshin, Tardi, & Tobin, 1966).

Specialized Research Facilities

The basic premise for putting a person in an institution must be that the professional staff of the comprehensive community center or equivalent clinic does not know what is needed to help him remain in his community. This would automatically make him a research subject and everything in the institution should be shaped to the end of developing the kinds of knowledge and experience to approach a solution to his problem (Bair & Leland, 1967). The institution would provide both a research setting and a training setting to help students of retardation develop increased professional knowledge while working under the supervision of career research and clinical people to solve the problems of retarded patients. This approach has been effective in other areas of science and is long overdue in behavioral science. Basic research, applied research, and problem solving should be going on under the same roof so that laboratory discoveries can be field-tested and applied to service programs without having to move to other geographical areas or to change the team or the kinds of patients involved. The major function of the residential institution thus would be a search for new problem solutions.

By focusing on the experimental aspect, the program would become truly patient-oriented, for its purpose then would be to find out the answers to the peculiar difficulties presented by each patient. Everything done with him from the time he got up in the morning until he went to bed at night would in a sense be an experiment (Barrett, 1971). When the institution could set up patterns to which the patient responded, they would be recorded, tested, and made part of the handbook of treatment. When he did not respond, the institution would try to find out why.

However, this research approach must always be tempered with a regard for the patient as a person. He must always be treated with dignity and "research" can never become an excuse for abandoning or negating any of his basic human rights.

For an institution to carry out this kind of program it must have three essential factors. There must be a large enough staff. They must have freedom to make mistakes. And there must be communication among all parts of the staff so that information can become cumulative.

There must be a large enough staff and an able enough staff to attract students and to provide them an effective learning situation. This would require that the institution be affiliated with a university or other seat of advanced learning, that the research-clinical personnel have university appointments, and that these scientist-academicians have sufficient stature that students would want to work with them. Therefore, whenever possible, residential institutions should be tied to the university-affiliated facilities (PL 88-164; PL 91-517).

When the state has taken over a person it has the responsibility of treating him, but we do not as yet know how to treat the patients who reach these centers; that is the very reason they come there. The centers have to search for the answers. During the searching they will find many blind alleys and many approaches that do not work. Freedom to make mistakes is an essential part of any training and research situation. Everybody at every level of contact with the patients has to be part of the research and training team and has to feel free to try special things and to learn to report the things they have tried, including the errors they have made, so that every single interaction with the patient becomes part of the research data. (Of course, any stringent or potentially hurtful treatment is tried only with the approval and under the supervision of the senior professionals.) Further, all procedures must, whenever possible, be followed only after the patient has given full, informed consent. When the functional level of the patient precludes such consent, it must be obtained from a parent, close relative, or guardian. Psychiatric aides under supervision of the nurses must carry on patient interaction, so as to free the professional staff for consultation rather than having them solely responsible for patient contact. This means that the aides must not only mop floors and the nurses must not devote most of their time passing out medication and giving shots; someone else should handle those functions. If this kind of approach is maintained within the institution, answers will be found and patients will be enabled to return to their communities much more quickly.

Everything done with the patient should be recorded and communicated. There must be frequent conferences and seminars which would include everyone who had day-to-day interaction with the patients. The whole group would be involved in reporting so that there could be an accumulative collection of data available to build up knowledge and eventually to help solve our problems.

This kind of productive research and professional training program cannot go on in the large general institutions of today. Only small, specialized institutions that handle homogeneous groups of problems can provide the right setting. Thus, for example, each state should have affiliated with its medical schools specialized pediatric services of no more than 25 beds per school. Pediatric specialists and professors with their students would be assigned to them to work with the children, who would remain in the institution while their problems were studied and would then be transferred back to their own homes with special provisions for continued care or to one of the care units. Similarly, we must have neurological centers of fifteen to twenty beds where the more unusual neurological disorders could be studied. Other similar specialized units of varying numbers of beds should be planned around orthopedic defects, sensory defects, etc.

In addition to these small, highly specialized centers, we would expect the development of **behavioral centers** that would be somewhat bigger but that would have no more than 150 to 200 beds. Here a large variety of specialists from many disciplines would be assigned from the university with their students. Among them would be child development and behavior modification specialists, specialists in direct clinical treatment—for example, speech and hearing, physical therapy, and occupational therapy—psychiatrists and psychologists, and a variety of physicians, dentists, social workers, nurses, and educators. The patients would be admitted to such institutions because of their maladaptive behavior; when the behavior was reversed or modified they would be discharged to other types of service facilities in their home communities, or sent back to their own homes; and the effective methods of treatment would be made known to all professionals who might be able to use them. No patient should remain in such a facility for more than three years regardless of his progress.

All of these institutions would have specific functions in regard to specific disorders, based on broad conceptions of the etiology of those disorders. In comparison with present institutions they would be very small so that the special study-research teams could be effective. The residential institution would become a laboratory, a place where problems could be examined, worked through, and where once success had been achieved the patients would be sent back to the community to live out their lives at a more normal level. Even in those cases where the study was not successful, enough would be learned in the three years to help other patients in the future.

Overseeing Agency Needed

As broad a program as this would need constant supervision and surveillance by some agency in each community. As we have discussed earlier, such an agency should provide club facilities to which retarded people could turn for support and advice (MacLeech, 1968), but more important, it should provide constant and regular citizen **advocacy** for the needs of retarded individuals. It should insure that funds are spent properly, that the special needs of the retarded are being met, and that where necessary new programs are established. It would become the overall guardian of the retarded segment of the population, thus providing the necessary separation between the facilities that provided services and the guardianship function. Only by such a division could conflicts of interest be avoided.

Once such an agency is formed it would have certain immediate responsibilities. The first would be to oversee the establishment of appropriate training, treatment, and care facilities within the community. The second would be to bar the doors of existing institutions to new admissions until the patients now in these institutions were discharged or redistributed into the other facilities. Then it should begin to examine and set priorities for any other moves that would make a retarded person's life more productive both to the community and to himself.

13

Prevention, Research, and Manpower

We have discussed the increasing body of knowledge about mental retardation. Now we must consider ways in which this knowledge can be used to prevent the condition, and when that is not yet possible, ways to press forward with research that will give us the best and most immediate results.

Four Kinds of Prevention

The idea of prevention has been approached in many ways. In the past, each agency or discipline involved has proposed measures based upon its own concerns, but an effective approach to prevention must be both inter-agency and multi-disciplinary. The major question that all agencies and disciplines must face is how the various elements that cause a high-risk situation (President's Panel, 1962) can be controlled.

In approaching this question it is useful to think in terms of the retarded person and his relationship to an external **host**—the individual or group with whom he lives—rather than restricting the concept of prevention to the primary individual. The host must be modified or rectified to reduce the high-risk element. Basically there are three kinds of host: maternal, familial, and communal. And there are four types of prevention: one, measures to prevent occurrence of the condition; two, measures to prevent its growth or extension;

three, measures to prevent compounding of its social implications; and four, measures to prevent later deterioration of the individual. This broad, panoramic scheme emphasizes that there is a continuous need for many kinds of preventive measures involving different social units rather than the seemingly futile search for specific, discrete actions that will prevent retardation once and for all.

When we consider the mother as host, we must first examine her biophysical ability to be a mother. Such considerations, to aid in prevention, must of necessity start before she conceives. Her nutritional state, her hormonal state, and her general protoplasmic pattern—her "mother power"—are what she brings to the conception of a new child, and they can have a very adverse effect on the development of the newborn. Both her own nutritional state and her **familial** nutritional history may have a distinct effect on the health of the infant (Winick, 1970). The baby can get nothing from the mother which she herself does not have. Nutritional deficiencies make it impossible for some mothers to transmit necessary elements to their infants, particularly if the elements that are lacking relate to protein intake and DNA production. She may also have diseases and other conditions that can lead to errors of metabolism (Stoller, 1968), or developmental errors leading to defects during the gestation period (Gentry, Parkhurst, & Bulin, 1959). In addition we know that a great number of medicines and drugs, ranging from the simple aspirin tablet to hard narcotics and barbituates, can have a damaging effect on an unborn child (Nachman, 1971). The medication that she takes to correct her ills may itself produce undesirable effects. To further complicate the matter, teratogenic agents—agents producing abnormal growths or monstrocities—have a differential effect, depending on the stage of fetal development at the time during which the **teratogene** is presented. Thus, certain elements such as vitamin A which are necessary for proper fetal development at one stage, cause problems if they are present in the wrong quantities at other stages (Kalter & Warkany, 1959).

There are still other difficulties of the gestation period known as intrauterine insults. These affect the unborn child

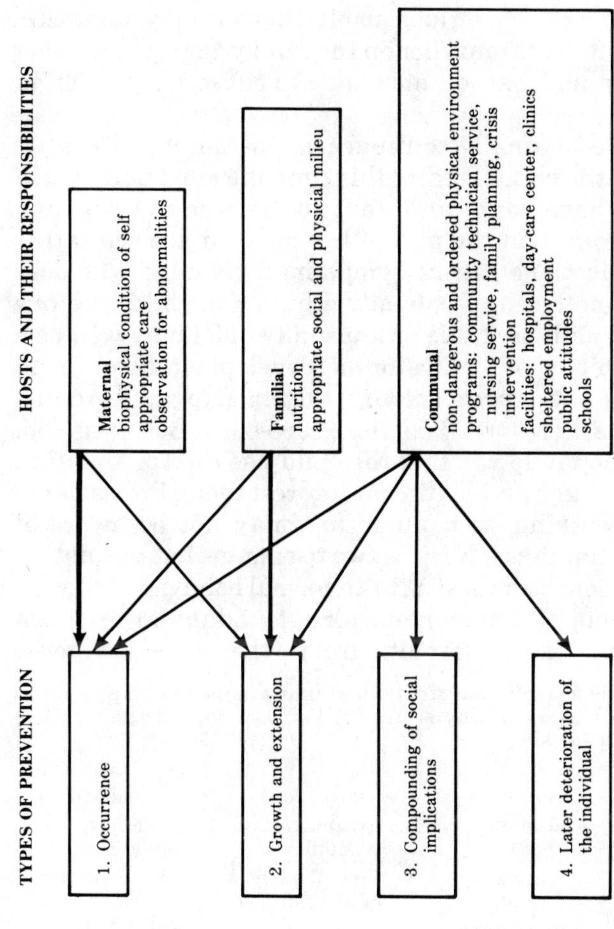

Figure 4. Types of Prevention, Hosts, and Host Responsibilities

detrimentally, and often originate completely outside the mother. Among them are irradiation, lead and other poisons (Overly, 1969), and viral diseases such as rubella (Cooper, 1966). The mother must be alerted to these and other dangers from normal daily living. She probably is aware, for example, that use of narcotics, excessive use of alcohol, or smoking can produce serious insults; but she may not realize that failure to fix the muffler on the family car could lead her to absorb enough carbon monoxide to cause retardation in her child.

The mother normally continues as host for a period after the birth of the child. During this time she must be aware of the normal behavior of an infant so that she can note any deviation from it on the part of her own child. Even rather general indications can be symptomatic: a child who does not accept mothering is already a high-risk child, and one who is unusually irritable or unusually quiet may well be a problem. One good indicator of developmental or birth problems is the Apgar scoring system (Apgar, Girdany, McIntosh, & Taylor, 1955, pp. 1985-88).[1] But it is not sufficient merely to say that the child has an Apgar within the normal range and let the matter rest there. Professional personnel working with an infant may not be aware of symptoms that take a week or two to emerge, but the mother can notice them if she is alert to abnormal behavior. After the baby is brought home he begins to adapt to an open environment (as different from the closed, sterile

[1]The Apgar is a brief scale of vital life signs that is applied as soon as possible after delivery. If any scores are low it is applied again in five minutes. The scale is:

	0	1	2
Heart rate	absent	below 100	100 or above
Respiratory effect	absent	irregular, slow, or shallow	good effort, lusty cry
Muscle tone	completely flaccid	some flexion of extremities	active motion
Reflex irritability	no response	grimace	cry
Color	blue, pale	body pink but extremities blue	completely pink

10 points are healthy. Anything less indicates problems. 5 points or less indicate high probability of death.

environment of the hospital). This need for adaptation brings new signs or behavioral elements to the fore. The mother should be provided with a guide of high-risk signs and expected social responses for the first six weeks of life.

During the post-natal period the mother's diet is still of importance. This is particularly true if she is nursing the baby (Heinstein, 1963), but even if she is not, her nutritional state contributes to her ability to ward off disease and her ability to maintain emotional stability. A well mother is much better able to cope with developing conditions than one who is generally below par or actually ill.

Considering the mother as host in terms of the four aspects of prevention, we find that her most important function is prevention of the occurrence of retardation. Her next most important one is prevention of its growth during the period immediately after birth. In her role as host she has little influence on the remaining two aspects, although at a later time as a member of society she may well have an effect upon them.

To perform her important functions as host, the woman who is to become a mother should understand the prevention of mental retardation at various steps in the process of motherhood. The first is during the pre-conception period, when she must prepare herself; the second is during the gestation period when she must protect and nurture the unborn child; and the third is during the immediate post-natal period, when she must both care for him properly and observe him carefully for any abnormal behavior (Gold, Stone, & Rich, 1969; Morris, Hatch, & Chapman, 1966). If she understands and follows these procedures, she should be an effective host for her child.

The child usually moves gradually from having his mother as sole host to having his family as host. Here by family we do not necessarily mean parents, brothers and sisters, but rather whatever people in the child's immediate surroundings he relies upon for survival and care. They are the ones who normally see him through the first four years of his life, a major period in this development because during this time his brain cells develop (first ten weeks) and grow and expand (next four years) at an accelerated rate.

During this period it is the family's responsibility to maintain an appropriate environment and provide the necessary raw materials for the physical, emotional, and intellectual development of the child. He will need proper nutrition, opportunity for sensory discrimination, and opportunity for sensory stimulation without inundation by the stimuli. The members of his family must all provide some emotional outlet for the child's need to be gentled, loved, talked to, and generally shown that they know he exists and are pleased with the idea. Further, there need to be certain individuals with whom he can develop a security relationship. The important thing here is to prevent physical, intellectual, or emotional growth blockage which can arise if the child is constricted in his efforts toward normal orientation in his environment. If the child does not have the proper family relationship, efforts must be made to create it, and failing that the child should be put in a foster or adopted home (Gallagher, 1968).

At the same time, the family must develop a protective environment around the child. Here we know specifically most of the things that should be prevented. He should have immunization against diseases, including such recent developments as immunization against rubella, polio, and measles. There must be proper home sanitation to control vermin, rodents, and other destructive organisms. The thought here is not to provide an absolutely sterile environment around the child—he should in fact have appropriate contact with normal dirt—but to protect him from viral diseases and those carried by animals, both of which are particularly destructive to a young child.

As he grows older, his protective environment must become more far-reaching. The family has to consider the physical dangers around the house—medicines, cleaning fluids, detergents, sharp objects, high and unsteady places, and so on—which may cause the child in his normal pattern of growth and exploration to damage himself permanently. Then as he begins to move outside the house they must broaden these considerations further, to include outdoor dangers such as traffic, dangerous trees, and overexposure to sun.[2] This protection should not, however, be maintained by constant policing of the child, as it will impede his opportunities for growth and development. Should he already have shown signs of mental retardation he probably will be surrounded by a family with a tendency to overprotect and overdefend him, but this tendency in itself can be damaging. Both neglect and overprotection can harm a child.

The family's responsibility is to insure that the child participates in normal living experiences as well as he is able. He must be permitted to reach out, to touch, to examine and generally to interact with his physical and social environment, yet at the same time be protected from dangers that are physically damaging—the hot stove, for example. His waking day should be loaded with new and exciting experiences; these might be such activities as moving about as much as is feasible, or playing with toys or pets with which he can interact on a highly personal basis.

Looking at the family as host in terms of the four aspects of prevention, it is clear that its main function is to prevent growth or extension of retardation and its second function is to prevent its occurrence. As a family it is not greatly involved in the other two aspects.

Most of a child's early maturational processes are centered around the family as a host. But once he learns to walk and begins to roam somewhat farther afield—going out into the yard to play, or even going out into the hallway of the tenement—he immediately passes from the environment controlled by his family into conditions mainly controlled by the community. Thus as he grows older, the community more and more becomes his primary host.

But the community has other responsibilities toward him that begin long before this time. The original endowment of the child is based on "mother power." Thus the most basic community preventive programs must be those that provide

[2]The American Academy of Pediatrics, 1801 Hinman Avenue, Evanston, Ill. 60204, has prepared a group of pamphlets in such areas as school safety, accident prevention, sex education, feeding and nutrition, etc., for the purpose of providing selected readings in these areas.

the mother physical analyses, psychological evaluations, corrections of positive findings, appropriate nutritional programs, and consultation on family processes. All will make her a better physical, social, and emotional host. The result will be an increase of well, healthy births and a decrease in the premature infants and infants with inborn errors of metabolism that become the most typical cases of retardation and developmental disability (President's Panel, 1962).

There is also a need for a visiting nursing service that will visit each newborn child shortly after he comes home. This should be a routine process, regardless of the family involved. If the nurse finds that everything is well taken care of and that the baby shows no signs of developmental anomaly, or that if he does the parents have taken appropriate steps, that family needs no further attention from her. But if there are problems or if there is a high-risk situation, she must then put the parents in touch with the agencies that can give the infant the best possible chance to develop.

Further, there must be a wide expansion of family planning agencies, not in order to maintain a program of child prevention, but to give people control over their own reproductive processes and to permit them to time and space births so as to use the highest potential of the family. This will require services to provide contraceptive information, sex education (SEICUS, 1971; Bass, Kempton, & Gordon, 1971), and abortion when needed or desired. Such abortions should be freely available on request, as should also be appropriate genetic and social counseling (Kaplan, 1969) so that the parents will have full understanding of the implications of bringing another child into their particular situation.

A primary aspect of community responsibility is to clean out sources of danger and disorder that are potential causes of handicaps for normal children and major causes of acerbation of the conditions of handicapped children. These sources may be garbage, insects and rodents, and such things as battery acid and lead. One source of lead poisoning is the lead-based paint that was formerly the best available, and was used on many of the good houses in old residential areas. These have since deteriorated, and the paint is now chipping and flaking on those same houses; in many poor areas young infants can pick up the paint chips and eat them. Prevention in this example, as in many of the others, is relatively simple: find the houses that still have lead-base paint, strip the paint, and repaint them.

As the child grows older he must be given proper training during the preschool period. It has become increasingly apparent that academic retardation can be prevented and physical problems can be corrected during this period. At the same time there is a constant need for child advocacy, for people and agencies dedicated to the prevention of developing problems.

The community also is responsible for schools and vocational centers. When we deal with a normal child this responsibility focuses on giving him an appropriate education and an outlet for after-school activities. But when we deal with a handicapped or developmentally disabled child, there are further responsibilities. One of the main ones has to do with community attitudes. To be handicapped is one thing; to have the whole community despising you because of your condition is something quite different. The stresses produced by such public attitudes can quite literally increase the retardation. If responsible people throughout the community, ranging from educators to employers, can help the public develop more accepting attitudes toward retarded youngsters, this in itself will save many children from increased retardation. One way of accomplishing this is for schools and employers to give each individual the opportunity to work at the level his ability will permit, while at the same time accepting him as a person with due respect regardless of his disability.

With adolescents and adults who are mentally retarded there is no question of preventing the condition, but there is a definite need to prevent the individuals' deterioration and their accompanying development of severe emotional disturbances that would require hospitalization or psychiatric treatment. The main answers again center on the schools. People cannot exist in a vacuum, yet the retarded also cannot perform in the same manner as their peers; so we must provide substitute activities for them. These can best be developed by the expansion of adult and vocational educational programs and also of training programs that help the retarded utilize their leisure time. Both kinds of programs should be the responsibility of the secondary schools.

The delivery of preventive services requires outreach programs carried on by specially trained community service technicians. These people must live in the areas where they work and must be acquainted with the other residents. In this way they can learn of developing problems and notify the appropriate agencies to take whatever corrective action is necessary.

There must be a considerable expansion in sheltered or contract workshops for the adolescent and adult retarded, because technological advances in industry and the presence in the community of more-able workers who are unemployed often make it difficult for retarded people to find normal jobs. Such workshops bring added economic resources to their communities; for example, a workshop that can do a minor job requiring a high degree of primitive specialization such as "tipping" in the printing industry can aid local businesses—in this case independent houses—in competing for contracts that otherwise they could not fulfill economically.

There also is a need for on-the-spot prevention through the process of **crisis intervention.** If a retarded person finds himself in a situation with which he cannot cope, and he is unable to receive the help that he needs, his subsequent breakdown may give the community a new problem. But if there is a "fixed point of reference," a telephone number, a local clubroom, or some similar source of advice readily available to him, his problem can usually be solved quite readily and he can go about his business without further difficulty.

The final community responsibility centers around hospitals, clinics, day-care centers, and similar establishments, where children are brought because they have "a condition." These facilities must constantly define the sources of any given child's problems; such sources may turn out to be destructive factors in the social ecology or events such as child abuse, "battering" or neglect, all of which must be reported and controlled (Poole, 1965). The hospital or clinic often becomes the first agency of change (Eichenwald, 1966), even though the disorder may not be of a biomedical or physical nature, by gathering information both about the causes of disorders and about possible areas of prevention (Schweitzer, 1969).

Thus when we consider the community as host in terms of the four aspects of prevention—measures to prevent occurrence, measures to prevent growth or extension, measures to prevent compounding of social implications, and measures to prevent later deterioration—we find that it has responsibilities for all of them.

There are three subdivisions of mental retardation programming; they are case management, correction, and prevention. The last has received the lowest national priority, yet it is the one that should receive top priority. Prevention programs should maintain a birth-to-death commitment. It is completely absurd, for example, to feel that the expense of helping a mother during gestation is unnecessary while at the same time spending millions of dollars for total care of children and adults who would never have been in the institutions in the first place if a relatively small amount had been spent on their mothers during their pre-natal periods. Prevention must come first.

Research: New Vistas

Recent research on mental retardation has opened up new vistas (Dingman, 1968) for further research and has shown us just how much remains to be done (Ellis, 1966, 1967, 1968, 1971). We not only need to give prevention the highest priority within the field of mental retardation, but we also need to give research the highest priority within our prevention effort. Basic research, applied research, and problem-solving research all must be expanded.

Basic research is needed upon the problems of sensory-motor development, of **cytogenics,** and of cognitive

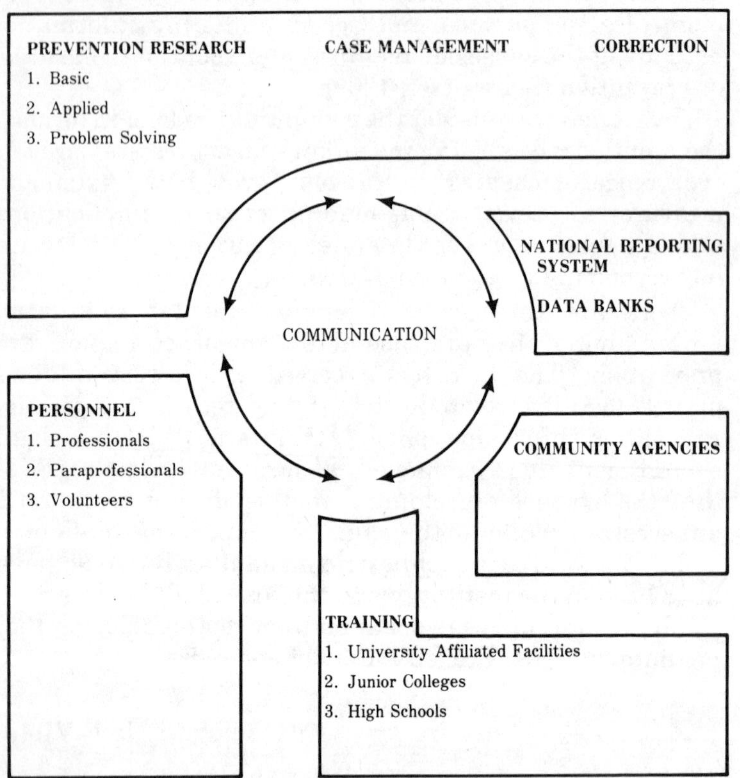

Figure 5. Mental Retardation Programming

development. In the cytogenic area we need to understand more about the DNA-RNA processes and the relationship between messenger RNA and nutritional and metabolic deficiencies. In the area of cognitive development we need to know more about memory processes, attention, orientation, and the development of emotions, decisions, strategy, and thought. (Haywood, 1968; Hermelin, 1968; Bijou & Baer, 1963; Thomas, Chess, Birch, Hertzig, & Korn, 1963; and Astrup, Sersen, & Wortis, 1967, all demonstrate types of approaches to basic research that are particularly useful at this time.)

We also need basic biochemical research into the roles of hormones, enzymes, and nutrients, and the whole broad aspect of finding out just what goes on inside the human body. The information developed by such research will help us determine how deficiencies can be prevented, and if they do occur how they can be alleviated. There is a need for basic research into the origin and nature of birth defects and their relationship to environmental forces. In all of these research areas we do not expect to find discrete causes of conditions, but rather we hope to learn enough that we can sort out the interlocking processes and understand how they contribute to etiologies that now appear as unified entities; here much of the work done with animals can make a useful and valuable contribution (Berkson, 1967).

The need for applied research is even greater because so little of it has been done. We must have more developmental research on how learning occurs (Bijou, 1968), on how appropriate coping processes develop, on how adaptive behavior matures, and on how social awareness evolves (Barclay, 1969; Bialer & Sternlicht, 1969). All of these elements contribute to the social and behavioral etiology of mental retardation (Foster & Nihira, 1969) and must be understood better if we are to control the condition.

Much money has been spent on community mental health and retardation centers, university affiliated centers, child-guidance clinics, etc. These centers should not only have a research emphasis but should also strive to improve the manner in which their research is carried on (Dinnerstein & Lowenthal, 1968; Gardner, 1969; Lucero, Vail, & Scherber,

1968). Their programs become meaningless unless they can share what they are doing with the rest of the country and unless they themselves know exactly what results they have achieved. To do this they must put much more emphasis on evaluating their own programs.[3]

This evaluation will probably show that many of the things they are doing are not producing results and that there are many new programs which should be tried. The new programs may or may not be successful, but negative results are often as useful as positive ones. Whatever the results, however, they must be disseminated so that something that develops in Columbus, Ohio, can be appropriately used in Parsons, Kansas; the system of locking up information in small capsules in minor geographical locations has become a serious problem. Data banks containing both behavioral and research information must be established, fed from all of the agencies that do this type of work, and made available to all other agencies and professionals in the field (Eyman, 1969).

Money and personnel for research are limited. We cannot say that a program is necessary and should therefore be developed without regard to cost. Instead, we must devise ways to do the necessary jobs within our means; as one step in this direction, we must stop doing things just because we have been doing them and consider if there are not more economical ways of reaching the same goals. But at the same time we must take into account psychological economics—the real meaning of value in terms of a healthy, more efficient society. Even so, a more appropriate distribution of training and service resources can give us both a sounder use of the funds available and better service to the handicapped. Thus the utilization of the model proposed in Chapter 8 (including family allotments, neighborhood service centers, comprehensive community centers, etc.) not only provide for better service delivery but also for more economical use of existing resources.

[3]Special attention should also be devoted to the ethical considerations of research with human subjects (*APA Monitor,* May, 1972).

In most colleges and professional schools today, specific training in the area of developmental disability is not available. The field of developmental disability needs an increased number of physicians, dentists, psychologists, social workers, occupational therapists, nurses, physical therapists, speech and audiology personnel, educators, vocational counselors, music therapists, recreation therapists, nutritionists, and members of other allied professions such as law, computer science, sociology, anthropology, and genetics. In addition, new orientation at the pre-baccalaureate level should produce such paraprofessionals as day-care workers, home trainers, infant educators, mental retardation aides, outreach workers, and home management aides. Every university discipline should give some consideration to students who might go into mental retardation as a sub-specialty; this is as true of chemistry and physics, where specialists are needed to work on cybernetic and biochemical questions, as it is of psychology, social work, and medicine, where graduates will work directly with retarded people. But often students who do want to go into the field are unable to get the necessary training.

One attempt to correct the situation has been the development of university affiliated centers. Through these centers students who are seeking professional training in MR can get both the general training in their discipline and the specific training in mental retardation as part of their regular college programs (Leland, Smith, & Barclay, 1970). Such centers can give intensive special attention to handicapped people who do not respond to the techniques now used (Haywood, 1970), and at the same time perform the training function on an interdisciplinary basis.

Facilities at universities that grant advanced degrees must work closely with community agencies and make the maximum use of the opportunities that they offer for practical training; this sort of training should be one of the requirements for the degree. If such a procedure can be followed, the professionals who come into the field to work with the retarded will have a higher degree of proficiency and a better knowledge of the area.

Manpower

It has become axiomatic that throughout their training students work with retarded clients, but once they have completed it they move into administrative planning, research, professional training, and other top-level activities. Thus a clinic is typically manned by student workers under doctoral-level supervisors. Such clinics give good service to the extent of their physical abilities and it has become increasingly clear that their clients can be served in routine manners just as well by people with less training as by those who have completed their professional training. In fact, the patients may be served better, because the less highly-trained worker will probably do his specific task—giving a psychological test, for example—thoroughly and appropriately, while the doctor who has had more intense professional training is likely to put his own variations into the task and thus not carry it out as systematically or efficiently (Davidson, 1965).

Professional manpower to staff the expanded facilities we need is in short supply and is also expensive (President's Committee, 1968). Therefore it seems logical that the new facilities be filled largely by paraprofessionals, trained in high schools and junior colleges to be specific kinds of technicians who do the more routine activities within their disciplines. This opens up a whole new area of career possibilities for people who are highly trained in very specific activities instead of in the general aspects of the discipline (Sutter, Leland, & Barclay, 1969). By using such technicians there need be fewer top professionals in any given facility, the more highly-trained personnel can concentrate upon the problems that require their special backgrounds and extensive training.

Financially it is far more economical to provide family allotments so that a mother can stay home and work with her children than it is to put money into residential institutions. A child who reveals behavioral and learning lags in the first three years of his life can be helped to reverse these lags if behavior shaping procedures are followed, and they can be followed readily within the home. (This is not to imply that the biomedical aspects can be reversed, but rather that the forms of behavior resulting from them can be reversed or modified at this early age.) Here again there is a need for well-trained paraprofessional home-training technicians who work with and train the mothers of retarded children.

Thus when the visiting nursing service described earlier finds that there is a problem with a newborn child it should be able to call upon a trainer who goes into the home, plans with the parents the modification programs needed, and shows the parents how to carry them out. The trainer can then return on a regular basis to guide the home training and to deal with any new problems that have emerged. In this way the traditional role of the parent as the person responsible for the early training of her child is maintained, but now she has advice and guidance in dealing with special problems of development.[4]

We can make good use of volunteers as well; they also offer a large and untapped manpower resource. There are many retired workers whose economic needs are secured by their pensions, but whose psychological needs for worthwhile activity are not at all fulfilled. Such workers with a minimum of training can provide a great deal of individual-to-individual support to older retarded people, who should have regular contact and intervention from able individuals but who do not necessarily need professional attention. Development of the big brother concept into what has been described as a foster grandparent program should be expanded so that more retired people can be trained to provide personal contact of this sort through an outreach program.

In Sum . . .

We now have enough knowledge to establish guidelines for mothers, families, and communities to fulfill their

[4]Personal communication, Ann S. Bardwell, Ph.D., Chief, Home Economics, Nisonger Center, The Ohio State University, 1971.

obligations of preventing conditions leading to mental retardation. The principles that have been outlined thus far in this chapter underline the need for making preventive programs the number one priority in the normalization process (see Figures 4 and 5).

In many important areas, however, our information is still insufficient or completely lacking. There is a great need for research in these areas. Coupled with this need is the responsibility of researchers to collect, store, and disseminate all available data and information. A uniform national reporting system and a network of data banks should be organized to accomplish this.

The need for increased numbers of trained personnel leads us also to take a new look at professional training programs. We see that such programs must include both extensive training for the preparation of mental retardation specialists and technical training at the pre-baccalaureate level. This latter paraprofessional training should include parents and other individuals who make up the child's social unit. The combination of prevention programs where we now have the knowledge, research programs where we need new knowledge, and training programs to provide the needed professionals and paraprofessionals will put us well on the road to improved welfare of our handicapped citizens.

14

Advocacy for Action

Though it has taken a long time, people in various parts of the country are becoming aware of the issues raised in this book. This awareness underlies the current demands that something be done, immediately. These demands are reflected in civil rights suits presently before the courts or in the process of being filed. A review of some of these cases can be found in *Confrontation and Change* (Cohen, 1971). The suits, which have brought the whole system under examination, indicate a high level of distress regarding the failure to maintain the right to treatment for mentally retarded persons. Current admission and discharge policies of institutions raise allied questions of peonage and exploitation of handicapped individuals. The suits bring into contention questions involving the general policies of the state and question the ability of the citizenry to be able to get a fair return for the tax money spent in the present system. The consideration of monetary expenditure is put alongside the moral and ethical values since the needs of human beings do not necessarily have a dollar and cents price.

A major purpose of this book is advocacy for human rights of the mentally retarded. Advocacy falls into two areas: one, *social advocacy* which seeks systemic changes in the concept of today's large residential institutions which are seen as destructive to retarded people and in the patterns of service delivery which are far from adequate and in no way meet the expressed needs of the handicapped. And two, *personal advocacy* which sets for each of us a goal that everything we do in relationship to mentally retarded or handicapped persons should help broaden their options and help lead them closer to a normal life pattern. This book, rather than just "viewing with alarm" and presenting the horror picture of the present situation, has tried to give an overview of what has occurred, some of the reasons why these practices have occurred, and what must happen to produce the kinds of changes we are recommending.

To review briefly, we have outlined the patterns of care, treatment, and training, as they exist today. We have shown where these mechanisms are outmoded, destructive to the personality of the individual, and how in addition, they create a vast waste of both human and material resources. Many of the methods considered effective fifty to a hundred years ago have not been changed or brought to meet modern needs, nor have they been made consistent with advances in knowledge. The tendency for society to sequester individuals whom they do not understand has been continued beyond the period when this kind of an approach serves any social value. The general-purpose institutions are still with us in increasing number, though with much smaller populations per unit; these facilities are maintained in the face of all logic which tells us that if something does not work it should be abandoned and something new should be tried. The outstanding features of this carryover from the past are neglect and **apathy** with a tendency to say that this is something we will think about tomorrow, because there are more pressing problems facing us today. Yet this tomorrow has been a long time coming and lives continue to be degraded and depersonalized.

However, during this same period, dedicated individuals have continued to research and investigate questions related to how handicapping conditions occur, who is mentally retarded, how his brain functions differently, what is a developmental disability, how it occurs, how can it be prevented, how the disability or handicap can be reversed, and what procedures and new approaches are required to make changes happen. Much of this research effort has been successful and today we know that many behaviors which society previously considered threatening or evil no longer need to be considered in those terms. We know that many conditions which were considered inherited and irreversible can be modified and that many other conditions can be prevented. We know that every handicapped person, regardless of the depth of the retardation, can be helped in some manner and that most individuals can be brought to some level of social contribution. The research experience and demonstration efforts of the last few years have given us a very rich lore of information which should be made more generally available so that it can become part of planning and policy making and we can continue to move forward.

In this book we have only skimmed the surface of the literature, but we have tried to bring to light the most pertinent issues.[1] We have offered a social advocacy program which the body politic of the community could begin adapting to the special needs within each community, remembering that the modification of exceptional behavior requires exceptional planning. But it also requires clear understanding that this exceptional planning must use the "normal" behavior within each community as the base line.

We have outlined an educational structure which we feel will meet the needs of the educationally handicapped, both those who are mentally retarded and those who have other educational disabilities. We have presented a neighborhood-based plan of service delivery which state organizations could adopt to correct current deficiencies and to come closer to meeting the needs for prevention and habilitation. These proposed plans are based on the maintenance and enhancement of the civil and personal rights of the individual. The basic planning unit should be as similar to the social unit as possible and thus a neighborhood service center should become the major point of reference and resource. We have suggested a need to widen the

[1]Rothstein (1971) provides an excellent sourcebook of readings and references of use to parents and professionals. The appendix covers broad areas of resource materials including: (1) the organizations interested in mental retardation; (2) survey of the literature on mental retardation; (3) journals in mental retardation; (4) bibliography of textbooks on mental retardation; (5) specialized biographical listings; (6) U.S. Government agency publications; and (7) an annotated listing of over 150 films on mental retardation, including sources for procurement.

responsibility of the home and to maintain the identification of the individual with his social unit by continuing him at home, providing for family allotments, providing for home training services and other kinds of special services that will help keep him integrated into his personal community. We have recognized that the special needs of handicapped persons suggest the logic of using a variety of approaches and alternative methods to modify the environment with an increasing need for different levels of involvement. We have suggested various residential alternatives such as group care homes, foster homes, and supervised boarding houses within the neighborhoods as well as community service centers and specialized treatment centers outside of the neighborhood for the more complicated kinds of problems.

We have suggested that the personal and social needs of the individual should receive greater emphasis and that the state's responsibility should be confined to control of standards and quality of programs, to provision of necessary funding and to the development of an evaluation structure to monitor practices within the neighborhoods without, at the same time, so controlling their function that those neighborhoods with special needs could not maintain their programs. We have recommended a dual relationship where the program priorities and procedures emerge upward from the broad social unit closest to the handicapped individual, his neighborhood; at the same time the review of standards and quality programs can be provided by the state downward. The interaction should provide both the improvement of quality and the elimination of depersonalizing organization. Greater emphasis on the individual as part of his neighborhood will also modify many of the current problems of peonage, failure to deliver services, and destruction of individual rights as occurs in programs which are completely controlled from the top and divorced from family and community.

These recommendations have been based primarily on the effort to broaden individual options and develop rehabilitation procedures as reflected by the considerations presented in the *Declaration of General and Special Rights* (1969). These considerations bring out 1) the maximization of the person through the opening of new pathways for retarded and handicapped individuals to find alternative ways of dealing with their own coping problems and of their meeting society's need to cope with them; 2) the concept that every handicap is in some way compensable and that society in its responsibility to maintain a livable environment for all of its citizens must help the handicapped individual find ways of developing compensability; 3) that society has an obligation to try to assimilate and accommodate all of its citizens rather than to reject or isolate them from the main lines of social interaction; 4) that while society has a right to expect normal behavior so that law and social organization can be maintained, it also has the responsibility to negotiate the limitations on the individual's degrees of freedom rather than arbitrarily imposing depersonalizing and dehumanizing controls upon the handicapped individual; 5) that the modern development and **growth** of civilization has brought us to a level that we can afford to begin thinking in terms of the human effectiveness and the human benefits of a program rather than concentrating on the levels of efficiency of such a program.

A program which does not consider human benefits is really less efficient and more costly than one which, though possibly more expensive in a monetary sense, is really less costly over time because it permits individuals to emerge as contributing members of society. Thus, we are suggesting that current analyses of cost on the basis of money spent be reorganized into an accounting procedure that takes into consideration cost benefit with a very clear understanding that those costs from which society does not derive human benefit are greater and more expensive than those from which such benefit does derive.

If these five points are to become viable, both the social and personal advocate must always be aware of the right of handicapped persons to maintain the same basic rights as other citizens in the same country of the same age. This is the "normalization principle" and, more simply stated, says that the fact of a handicap or the fact of mental retardation should not of itself demand that the person live in an abnormal manner. Rather, the nature of the handicap, the extent of the retardation, has to become the guide as to what kinds of decision making, what kinds of social expectations, etc., can be met by the individual and the planning that goes forward around him has to be centered on those guides. Thus, for example, if he goes to a special school there is no real reason that he has to go in a specially marked vehicle; if he requires a residential alternative away from his own home, there is no reason why such alternatives should not have a home-like atmosphere, and there is no reason why the care personnel should have to wear uniforms, etc. The fact of retardation needing special programming does not require special markings on a bus or uniforms on individuals providing care. These kinds of considerations become the personal responsibility of each of us. This goes beyond the question of broad social advocacy and centers around each of our daily activities as we come into contact with mentally retarded and developmentally disabled persons. We have to be sure in our own hearts and minds that we are broadening every possible option. We must remember that there is no such thing as choice or freedom unless there are alternatives. We have to make very sure that we are constantly keeping those alternatives open so that the person may make his decisions along his lines. Then we can help him learn how to make socially acceptable decisions so as to guarantee his being a part of the ongoing social unit.

This book hopefully will be a challenge to each reader to go forward as an advocate to help create the necessary action steps that are required to bring this program to fruition. It becomes a further challenge to each reader to insure that they themselves, again in the words of the *Declaration of General and Special Rights* (1969), always, at all times, treat the retarded, the developmentally disabled, and the handicapped persons of our world with "sincere respect and personal regard."

Glossary

Special Terms Used in this Book and the More Common Terms in the Psychology of Mental Retardation

ABERRATION: any handicapping abnormality.

ABSTRACT (BEHAVIOR, IDEAS, INTELLIGENCE, ETC.): symbolic, the ability to manipulate or use symbols and concepts in dealing with unfamiliar problems. Antithesis of concrete which refers to particularized ideas and the manipulation of things.

ACCEPTANCE: permitting the expression of feelings without fear of reproach.

ACHIEVEMENT, ACADEMIC: the level of skill attained in education or school activities.

ACTIVITY THERAPY: the use of activities typically associated with leisure for therapeutic goals; e.g., athletics, arts and crafts, music.

ADAPTIVE BEHAVIOR: the manner in which the individual copes with the natural and social demands of his environment. viz. intelligence.

ADJUSTMENT: a state of harmony and adaptation; a relationship (as to the environment, other persons, etc.).

ADVOCACY, PERSONAL-SOCIAL: constant support for the continuous upgrading and advancement of human welfare. Personal advocacy refers to pleading on behalf of individuals, social advocacy refers to pleading on behalf of classes of persons.

AFFECT: a broad term including emotion, feeling, mood and the ability to relate to others.

AGE, CHRONOLOGICAL (CA): actual age of the individual in years and months.

AGE, EQUIVALENT (AE): the age for which a given score on a test of physical and social development is considered average or normal.

AGE, MENTAL (MA): the age for which a given score on an intelligence test is considered average or normal.

AGENESIS: failure of development, e.g., cerebral agenesis is failure of parts of the brain to develop.

AGGRESSION: attack, self-assertion, officiousness—the first or offensive attack.

AMBIVALENCE: contradictory feelings and motives directed simultaneously toward the same person or situation.

AMERICAN ASSOCIATION ON MENTAL DEFICIENCY (AAMD): leading multi-disciplinary professional organization in the field of mental retardation. Publishes *American Journal of Mental Deficiency* and *Mental Retardation.*

ANOMALY: any obvious deviation from prototype.

ANOXEMIA: reduction of oxygen content of the blood to a level insufficient to maintain adequate functioning of tissue.

ANOXIA: deficiency of oxygen.

ANTICONVULSANT: an agent which acts to prevent seizures.

ANXIETY: restlessness, agitation, and general distress due to the dread either real or unreal of being helpless in a hostile environment.

APATHY: morbid indifference.

APGAR SCALE: a measurement of the vital life signs of the newborn.

ASSESSMENT: measurement or evaluation of an individual in terms of preconceived criteria.

ATROPHY: degeneration of tissues.

AUTISM: morbid preoccupation with oneself. Characterized by severe withdrawal, and inappropriate responses to external stimulation.

BATTERED CHILD: refers to the symptoms and physical damage associated with prolonged or chronic incidents of child abuse or "battering."

BEHAVIOR: any activity of the organism whether physiological, psychological, or social.

BEHAVIOR MODIFICATION: any planned program to increase the behavioral repertoire of the individual and bring all behaviors under appropriate stimulus control.

BEHAVIORAL CENTER: a treatment center designed to deal primarily with problems of maladaptive behavior and poor social adjustment.

BINET TEST (STANFORD-BINET): a standardized test of general intelligence, which is administered individually. It has been criticized because of its cultural loading and high verbal demands.

BIOMEDICAL: refers to that segment of handicapping conditions which are caused by known or probable biological error. See also: Error.

BIRTH INJURY: injury to the individual during or immediately after the birth process.

BRAIN INJURY: various types of undifferentiated central nervous system disorders or damage; brain damage.

BRAIN LESION: the alteration of the structure of function of the brain due to injury or trauma.

CARDIAC: pertaining to the heart.

CASE HISTORY: reconstruction of the past life of an individual.

CENTRAL NERVOUS SYSTEM (CNS): the brain and the spinal cord.

CEREBRAL PALSY: impairment of motor functioning associated with brain dysfunction.

CEREBRAL TRAUMA: brain injury as a result of some type of physical force, e.g., a concussion.

CHAOS: See Sensory Chaos.

CHILD DEVELOPMENT CENTERS: a program to prevent, solve, modify, and investigate problems related to child growth and development for handicapped and economically disadvantaged children.

CHROMOSOMAL ERROR: failure of the chromosomes to reproduce an expected configuration, a presumed cause of those conditions said to be genetically based. See also: Error.

CHROMOSOME: the bodies in the cell nucleus which carry the genes (hereditary factors). See also: RNA, DNA.

CLINICAL SERVICES: services provided to relieve, treat, modify, and manage recognized diseases and conditions through procedures and interventions consistent with the ethical requirements of the profession.

CNS DYSFUNCTION (NEUROLOGICAL ERROR): presumed cause of those conditions said to be neurologically based. See also: Error.

COGNITION: a generic term for human behaviors which include thought, ideation, apperception, recognition, memory, reasoning, generalization, judgment, awareness, symbolic representation, abstraction, foresight, hindsight, and insight. See also: Perception, reception, intelligence.

COGNITIVE IMPOTENCY: the inability to adapt appropriate cognitive or coping strategies for decision making, problem solving, or social response.

COMPENSATION: the process of making up for a deficiency, either physical or psychological.

COMPREHENSION: act of understanding; usually refers to a level or degree of understanding in a particular area of functioning, for example, level of reading comprehension.

COMPREHENSIVE COMMUNITY SERVICE CENTERS: a program serving a catchment population of approximately 125,000-150,000. Provides expanded and intensive services to the handicapped in an interdisciplinary setting. Serves those individuals who are unable to benefit from more local services. See also: Neighborhood service center.

CONGENITAL: any condition which exists at birth.

CONTACT: to be in touch with objective reality.

CONTRACT WORKSHOP: a form of sheltered employment. See also: Sheltered workshop.

CONVULSIVE DISORDER: See Epilepsy.

COPE: the development of behavioral strategies for survival. May be thought of positively or negatively in terms of the success of the strategies.

COUNSELING: the relationship in which an individual receives help or finds an opportunity to release negative feelings and thus clear the way for adaptive growth.

CRISIS INTERVENTION, DIRECT: immediate intervention to relieve an emergency. Crisis intervention should be one of the responsibilities of all service delivering agencies.

CUES, ENVIRONMENTAL: stimuli and behavioral guides critical to the successful comprehension of environmental demands.

CULTURAL-FAMILIAL: refers to individuals diagnosed as mentally retarded in the absence of indications of cerebral pathology, but where there is a history of familial intellectual subnormality and cultural deprivation.

CULTURE: the mores, folkways, institutions, and traditions which distinguish one group or nation from another.

CYTOGENETIC (CYTOGENIC): pertaining to the development and differentiation of cells. Related to problems surrounding questions of chromosomal error. See also: Chromosomal error.

DAY CARE CENTERS: as used in this book, programs of special training and developmental stimulation for preschool children demonstrating developmental delay.

DEPRIVATION, ENVIRONMENTAL: reduction or lack of environmental stimulation and of opportunities for acquiring knowledge ordinarily provided young children.

DEVELOPMENT: the process of mental and/or physical maturation of an organism.

DEVELOPMENTAL ANOMALY: a malformation due to the failure or blockage of normal fetal development. See also: Intrauterine insult.

DEVELOPMENTAL MILESTONE: a discrete stage of growth or function which must occur for later stages to develop properly.

DIAGNOSIS: assessment based on structural observations and tests including: 1) previous history, 2) field observations of behaviors or symptoms, 3) expected behaviors for age group and cultural group, and 4) developmental expectations.

DIAGNOSIS, DIFFERENTIAL: refers to the effort to create classification differences between interrelated processes and conditions.

DISABILITY, DEVELOPMENTAL: under the provisions of federal legislation, includes mental retardation, cerebral palsy, epilepsy or other neurological conditions closely related to mental retardation, or which require treatment similar to that required for mentally retarded individuals.

DISABILITY, READING: a specific incompetency in reading, used to refer to a reading level below that expected on the basis of level of general intelligence and age.

DISADVANTAGED: used to describe the factors associated with poverty and want. See also: Deprivation, environmental.

DNA (deoxyribonucleic acid): the hereditary substance and prime carrier of heredity; principal constituents of chromosomes. See also: RNA, chromosomes.

DOWN'S SYNDROME (MONGOLISM): a congenital condition characterized by a flat skull, oblique eyeslit, stubby fingers and thumbs, and a variety of other typical stigmata. Usually includes marked arrest of physical and mental development. Associated with chromosomal error.

DYSGENESIS: failure of maturation, e.g., cerebral dysgenesis is failure of parts of the brain to mature as expected or to deteriorate.

EDUCABLE MENTALLY RETARDED (EMR): a term used to refer to mentally retarded persons who are capable of some degree of achievement in traditional academic subjects such as reading and arithmetic. Also used to refer to those mentally retarded children who may be expected to maintain themselves independently in the community as adults, or to that group of mentally retarded obtaining IQ scores between 50 and 80.

EEG (electroencephalograph): a polygraph method of charting brain activity by electric currents.

ENCEPHALITIS (ENCEPHALOPATHY): inflammation of the brain resulting from the response of the cerebral tissue to a wide variety of infections and toxins.

ENURESIS: bed-wetting.

EPILEPSY: convulsive disorder also known as cerebral dysrhythmia. Among others, *Grand mal* produces heavy seizures; *Petit mal* light seizures; *Jacksonian* localized muscle spasms based on focal damage to the brain.

ERROR: generic term used to identify atypical development or organization of the various body systems or their processes, e.g., neurological error, chromosomal error, developmental error.

ETIOLOGY: causative factors which result in a disorder, e.g., the etiology of some types of mental retardation is encephalitis.

FAMILIAL TRAIT: a characteristic which appears in successive generations of a family and which may be due to genetic or cultural influences.

FAMILY ALLOTMENTS: in this context, special funds to be made available to each family caring for a developmentally disabled person. See also: Developmentally disabled.

FRUSTRATION: the condition of being thwarted in the satisfaction of a goal. This sometimes results in aggressive, hostile acts.

GERIATRIC CENTER: a program of services and activities, both residential and non-residential, to modify and retard the destructive processes of aging.

GERIATRICS: refers to aging and the problems of the aged.

GESTALT: a total pattern based on an integration of separate parts into an independent whole.

HANDED EXPERIENCE: developed from the anthropological maxim "the hand is the father of the brain." Refers to the concept that learning originates in doing. See also: Sensory-motor development.

HANDICAP, MENTAL: a term used sometimes as a synonym for mental retardation. It is also used to refer to a specific or segmental defect in intelligence or other aspects of behavior.

HANDICAP, PRIMARY: refers to conditions considered direct causal agents of the handicap, e.g., Down's Syndrome, psychosis.

HANDICAP, SECONDARY: refers to conditions considered indirect causal agents of the handicap, e.g., malnutrition, hearing loss.

HOME TRAINERS: persons specially trained in child development, home management, public health, and special education to work with the handicapped person in his own home. Also trained to assist parents to work with their own children.

HOST: the state of affording sustenance, lodgment, or support to a developing organism.

HYDROCEPHALUS: an excess of cerebrospinal fluid in the ventricles of the brain; "water-on-the-brain."

HYPERACTIVE: intense, driven, restless activity (hyperkinesis).

HYPERSENSITIVE (HYPERDISTRACTABLE): a state of over-vigilance and constant shifts of attention priorities.

IMPAIRMENT, SENSORY: any damage or dysfunction of the special senses such as the visual or auditory apparatus.

IMPULSIVENESS: acting suddenly without foresight or prudence.

INDEPENDENT FUNCTIONING: the ability to successfully accomplish tasks or activities demanded by the general community, including critical survival demands for that community and typical expectations for specific ages.

INSTITUTION, GENERAL RESIDENTIAL: eleemosynary facilities established for the care, treatment, and custody of the mentally retarded. Synonyms: state schools, state hospital and training centers, state homes, children's colonies.

INTELLIGENCE: a multitude of interdependent factors which, when operating as a unit, direct the individual's mental behavior (in this book includes sensory-motor development, cognition, adaptive behavior, social intelligence, and rate of previous learning).

INTELLIGENCE QUOTIENT (IQ): originally the ratio of mental age to actual (chronological) age as measured by standardized tests; currently a measure based on the difference between an obtained score and the score normal for the person's age.

INTERVENTION: the application of techniques and procedures designed to improve or control ongoing behavior.

INTRAUTERINE INSULT: a foreign agent introduced during the gestation period (particularly during the first trimester) which injures or interfers with proper fetal development.

LEARNING DISORDER: any condition related to severe academic deficiency which cannot be explained otherwise. Usually associated with minimal brain dysfunction.

LETHARGY: an involuntary drowsiness or stupor.

LIFE PLAN: a coordinated design for dealing with the needs of a handicapped person from birth through death.

LUCIDITY: clearness, used to describe periods of reality contact between psychotic episodes.

MALINGERING: pretending illness or defect.

MATURATION: the process of biological and psychological development of the organism.

MEMORY: retention, the ability to recall previous experiences and sensation.

MEMORY BANK (ASSOCIATION BANK): a group of brain cells which allow for retention of information that enables the organism to know that certain stimuli have occurred previously.

MENTAL RETARDATION: refers to significantly subaverage general intellectual functioning existing concurrently with deficits in adaptive behavior, and manifested during the developmental period. Mental retardation is an inclusive term incorporating all that has been meant in the past by mental deficiency, feeblemindedness, dementia, oligophrenia, etc.

MINIMAL BRAIN DYSFUNCTION: a relatively mild impairment of brain functioning that subtly affects perception, learning, and behavior, without reducing overall intellectual potential.

MONGOLISM: See Down's Syndrome.

MOTHER POWER: the internal biological and psychological resources available to a woman at the time she conceives.

NEGATIVISM: tendency to do the opposite of what is expected or ordered.

NEIGHBORHOOD SERVICE CENTER (NSC): a program serving a catchment population of approximately 25,000-30,000. Responsible for area planning, distribution of family allotments, assignment of home trainers, outreach workers, and organization of residential services where needed, e.g., foster homes, nursing homes, etc.

NEONATE: a term applied to an infant from birth to one month of age.

NEUROLOGICAL ERROR: See CNS dysfunction.

NEUROSIS: the expression of an emotional conflict which reduces the effectiveness of the individual's functioning but in which there is little loss of contact with reality.

NORMALIZATION: a concept emphasizing that the handicapped person should have the same basic rights as other citizens of the same country and the same age. These include among others the same access to resources, the same opportunities for economic security, the same right to belong, the same privilege of guardianship, the same access to protection, and the same rights to legal representation.

ORGANICITY: describes a condition that can be indicated as being of physical origin, e.g., brain lesion.

TREATMENT: the process of helping the handicapped person develop new coping strategies and reorder existing knowledge and abilities into more acceptable modes. See also: Training.

TSI: Test of Social Inference. See also: Social inference.

UNIVERSITY AFFILIATED FACILITY (UAF): interdisciplinary professional training centers developed to demonstrate innovative methods of service delivery and research in developmental disability and to train specialists to work in this area.

VISIBILITY: unusual behaviors or appearances which depart from comformity or expectations and bring challenges, derision, or rejection from peers or other social groups.

WECHSLER TESTS: the Wechsler Adult Intelligence Scale (WAIS); or the Wechsler Intelligence Scale for Children (WISC). Has been criticized primarily because of its cultural bias.

References

Achenbach, T., & Zigler, E. Cue-learning and problem-learning, strategies in normal and retarded children. *Child Development,* 1968, **38,** 827-848.

Alexander, F. G., & Selesnick, S. T. *The history of psychiatry.* New York: Harper & Row, 1966.

American Academy of Pediatrics. *Bibliographic series.* Evanston, Ill.: American Academy of Pediatrics, 1963, 1965, 1968.

American Association on Mental Deficiency. *Directory of residential facilities for the mentally retarded.* Washington, D. C.: AAMD, 1968.

American Guidance Service. *Tests in educational materials catalogue.* Circle Pines, Minn.: AGS, 1970.

American Psychiatric Association. *Diagnostic and statistical manual of mental disorders.* (2nd ed.), DSM II. Washington, D. C.: American Psychiatric Association, 1968.

American Psychological Association. *Monitor.* Washington, D. C.: APA, 1971, **2**(7).

Apgar, V., Girdany, B. R., McIntosh, R., & Taylor, H. C. Neonatal anoxia I: A study of the relation of oxygenation at birth to intellectual development. *Pediatrics,* 1955, **15,** 1985-1988.

Apgar, V. A proposal for a new method of evaluation of the newborn infant. *Anesthesia and Analgesia,* 1953, **32,** 260-267.

Appell, M. J., & Tisdall, W. J. Factors differentiating institutionalized from non-institutionalized referred retardates. *American Journal of Mental Deficiency,* 1968, **73**(3), 424-432.

Argy, W. T. Montessori versus orthodox: A study to determine the relative improvement of the preschool child with brain damage, trained by one of the two methods. *Rehabilitation Literature,* 1968, **26**(10), 294-304.

Arnold, I. L., & Goodman, L. Homemaker services to families with young retarded. *Children,* 1966, **13**(4), 149-152.

Astrup, C., Sersen, E. A., & Wortis, J. Conditional reflexes, studies in mental retardation: A review. *American Journal of Mental Deficiency,* 1967, **72**(4), 513-530.

Baer, D. M., Peterson, R. F., & Sherman, J. H. The development of imitation by reinforcing behavioral similarity to a model. *Journal of Experimental Analysis of Behavior,* 1967, **10,** 405-416.

Baer, D. M., & Sherman, J. H. Reinforcement control of generalized imitation in young children. *Journal of Experimental Child Psychology,* 1964, **1,** 37-49.

Bair, H. V., & Leland, H. Management of the geriatric mentally retarded patient. *Mental Hospitals,* 1959, **10**(5), 9-12.

Bair, H. V., & Leland, H. Utilization and design of physical facilities for rehabilitation of mentally retarded. Final Project Report, July 1967, Parsons State Hospital and Training Center, Parsons, Kansas, Grant RD 1319, Vocational Rehabilitation Administration.

Baller, W. R. Conditioned response treatment for enuresis. *Exceptional Children,* 1956, **22,** 233-247.

Bandura, A. Behavioral psychotherapy. *Scientific American,* 1967, **216**(3), 78-86.

Baratz, J. C. Language and cognitive assessment of Negro children: Assumption and research needs. *Journal of the American Speech and Hearing Association,* 1969, **11**(3), 87-91.

Baratz, J. C., & Shuy, R. W. (Eds.) *Teaching black children to read.* Washington, D. C.: Center for Applied Linguistics, 1969.

Barclay, A. Longitudinal changes in intellectual and social development of non-institutionalized retardates. *American Journal of Mental Deficiency,* 1969, **73**(5), 831-837.

Barrett, B. H. Acquisition of operant differentiation and discrimination in institutionalized retarded children. *American Journal of Orthopsychiatry,* 1965, **35,** 862-885.

Barrett, B. H. Behavioral differences among an institution's backward residents. *Mental Retardation,* 1971, **9**(1), 4-9.

Barrett, B. H., & Lindsley, O. R. Deficits in acquisition of operant discrimination and differentiation shown by institutionalized retarded children. *American Journal of Mental Deficiency,* 1962, **67,** 424-436.

Bass, M., Kempton, W., & Gordon, S. *Love, sex, and birth control for the mentally retarded.* Philadelphia: Planned Parenthood Association on Southeast Pennsylvania, 1971.

Bateman, B. Learning disabilities—yesterday, today, and tomorrow. *Exceptional Children,* 1964, **31,** 166-177.

Baumeister, A. A. Learning abilities of the mentally retarded. In A. A. Baumeister (Ed.), *Mental retardation.* Chicago: Aldine, 1967.

Baumeister, A. A. Behavioral inadequacy and variability of performance. *American Journal of Mental Deficiency,* 1968, **73**(3), 477-483.

Baumeister, A. A., & Hawkins, W. F. Alpha responsiveness to photic stimulation on mental defectives. *American Journal of Mental Deficiency,* 1967, **72**(5), 783-786.

Baylor Rubella Study Group. Rubella: Epidemic in retrospect. *Hospital Practice,* 1967, **2**(3), 27-35.

Beier, D. C. Behavioral disturbances in the mentally retarded. In H. Stevens & R. Heber (Eds.), *Mental retardation.* Chicago: University of Chicago Press, 1964.

Bender, L. *A Visual Motor Gestalt Test and Its Clinical Use.* American Orthopsychiatric Association, 1938, No. 3.

Bender, L. Psychological problems of children with organic brain disease. *American Journal of Orthopsychiatry,* 1949, **19,** 404-414.

Bensberg, G. J. *Teaching the mentally retarded: A handbook for ward personnel.* Atlanta: Southern Regional Education Board, 1965.

Bensberg, G. J., Colwell, C. N., & Cassell, R. H. Teaching the profoundly retarded self-help activities by behavior shaping techniques. *American Journal of Mental Deficiency,* 1965, **69**(5), 674-679.

Berkson, G. Aspects of a comparative psychology of mental deficiency. *American Journal of Mental Deficiency,* 1967, **72**(1), 10-15.

Berlyne, D. E. Soviet research on intellectual processes in children. In J. C. Wright, & J. Kagan (Eds.), *Basic cognitive processes in children.* Monographs of the Society for Research in Child Development, 1963, **28**(2).

Bessell, H. The content is the medium: The confidence is the message. *Psychology Today,* 1968, **1**(8), 32-35, 61.

Bialer, I. Psychotherapy and other adjustment techniques with the mentally retarded. In A. A. Baumeister (Ed.), *Mental retardation: Selected problems in appraisal and treatment.* Chicago: Aldine, 1967.

Bialer, I. Relationship of mental retardation to emotional disturbance and physical disability. In H. C. Haywood (Ed.), *Social-Cultural aspects of mental retardation.* New York: Appleton-Century-Crofts, 1969.

Bialer, I., & Sternlicht, M. Psychological issues in mental retardation: Report of a survey. *Mental Retardation,* 1969, **7**(4), 35-37.

Bijou, S. W. Behavior modification in the mentally retarded: Application of operant conditioning principles. In H. Grossman (Ed.), *The pediatric clinics of North America: Mental retardation.* Philadelphia: W. B. Saunders, 1968, **15**(4).

Bijou, S. W. Research on the academic education of the retarded. In G. A. Jervis (Ed.), *Expanding concepts in mental retardation.* Springfield, Illinois: Charles C Thomas, 1968.

Bijou, S. W., & Baer, D. M. Some methodological contributions from a functional analysis of child development. In L. P. Lipsett & C. C. Spiker (Eds.), *Advances in child development and behavior.* Vol. I. New York: Academic Press, 1963.

Bijou, S. W., Birnbrauer, J. S., Kidder, J. D., & Tague, C. Programmed instruction as an approach to the teaching of reading, writing and arithmetic to retarded children. *Psychological Record,* 1966, **16**(4), 505-522.

Birch, H. G. *Brain damage in children.* Philadelphia: Williams & Wilkinns, 1964.

Birnbrauer, J. S., Bijou, S. W., Wolfe, M. M., & Kidder, J. D. Programmed instruction in the classroom. In L. P. Ullman, & L. Krasner (Eds.), *Case studies in behavior modification.* New York: Holt, Rinehart & Winston, 1965.

Birnbrauer, J. S., & Sawler, J. Token reinforcement for learning. *Mental Retardation,* 1964, **2,** 275-279.

Blackman, L. S., & Capobianco, R. J. An evaluation of program instruction with the mentally retarded utilizing teaching machines. *American Journal of Mental Deficiency,* 1965, **70**(2), 262-269.

Blackman, L. S., & Siperstein, G. N. Job analysis and vocational evaluation of the mentally retarded. *Rehabilitation Literature,* 1968, **29**(4), 103-105.

Blatt, B. *Exodus from pandemonium.* Boston: Allyn & Bacon, 1970.

Bortner, M. & Birch, H. G. Cognitive capacity and cognitive competence. *American Journal of Mental Deficiency,* 1970, **74**(6), 735-744.

Boston, J. A., Jr. The defective child, his family, and the use of a child guidance clinic. *American Journal of Public Health,* 1960, **50**(6), 799-802.

Bricker, W. A. Identifying and modifying behavioral deficits. *American Journal of Mental Deficiency,* 1970, **75**(1), 16-21.

Browning, R. M. Effects of irrelevant peripheral visual stimuli on discrimination learning in minimally brain damaged children. *Journal of Consulting Psychology,* 1967, **31**(4), 371-376.

Browning, R. M., & Shaver, D. O. *Behavior modification in child treatment.* Chicago: Aldine, 1970.

Burt, C. The genetic determination of differences in intelligence: A study of monozygotic twins reared together and apart. *British Journal of Psychology,* 1966, **57,** 137-153.

Carter, C. L., Hamerton, J. L., Polani, P. E., Gunlap, A., & Weller, S. D. V. Chromosome translocation as a cause of familial mongolism. *Lancet,* 1960, **11,** 678-680.

Carter, C. O., & Evans, A. A. Risk of parents who have had one child with Down's Syndrome (Mongolism) having another child similarly affected. *Lancet,* 1961, **11,** 785-787.

Chalfant, J. C., & Scheffelin, M. A. *Central processing dysfunctions in children: A review of research.* National Institute of Nervous Diseases and Stroke, 1969, No. 9.

Children's House. Cincinnati, Ohio: Children's House, 1970.

Cleland, C. C., & Swartz, J. D. Work deprivation as motivation to work. *American Journal of Mental Deficiency,* 1969, **73**(5), 703-712.

Cleland, J. *Fanny Hill.* New York: Valhalla Books, 1963, (1749).

Clements, S. D. *Minimal brain dysfunction in children: Terminology and identification.* Washington, D. C.: Dept. of Health, Education, and Welfare, National Institute of Neurological Diseases and Blindness, No. 3, 1966.

Cohen, J. S. Vocational rehabilitation of the mentally retarded: The sheltered workshop. In J. Rothstein (Ed.), *Mental retardation readings and resources.* (2nd ed.) New York: Holt, Rinehart & Winston, 1971.

Cohen, J. (Ed.) *Confrontation and change.* Ann Arbor: University of Michigan, 1971.

Coleman, R. D., & Stoller, A. A survey of mongoloid birth in Victorian Australia, 1942-1957. *American Journal of Public Health,* 1962, **52**(5), 813-829.

Conant, J. B. *Slums and suburbs.* New York: McGraw-Hill, 1961.

Conover, J. V. Community day care programs for severely and profoundly retarded children. In J. Rothstein (Ed.), *Mental retardation readings and resources.* (2nd ed.) New York: Holt, Rinehart & Winston, 1971.

Cook, J. J. A conceptual framework within which to view adaptive behavior in the retarded. *American Journal of Mental Deficiency,* 1966, **71**(1), 64-72.

Cooper, L. Z. German measles. *Scientific American,* 1966, **215**(7), 30-37.

Cowan, P. A., Hoddinott, B. A., & Wright, B. A. Compliance and resistance in the conditioning of autistic children: An explanatory study. *Child Development,* 1965, **36,** 913-923.

Crome, L., & Stern, J. *The pathology of mental retardation.* London: J. & A. Churchill, Ltd., 1967.

Crosson, J. E. A technique for programming sheltered workshop environments for training severely retarded workers. *American Journal of Mental Deficiency,* 1969, **73**(5), 814-818.

Crosson, J. E., Youngberg, D. C., & White, O. W. Transenvironmental programming: An experimental approach to the rehabilitation of the retarded. In H. J. Prehm (Ed.), *Rehabilitation research in mental retardation,* No. 2. University of Oregon, 1970.

Davidson, G. C. The training of undergraduates as social reinforcers for autistic children. In L. P. Ullman, & L. Krasner, *Case studies in behavior modification.* New York: Holt, Rinehart & Winston, 1965.

Declaration of general and special rights of the mentally retarded. *Mental Retardation,* 1969, **7**(4).

Deutsch, A. *The mentally ill in America.* (2nd ed.) New York: Columbia University Press, 1952.

Deutsch, M. Facilitating development in the preschool child. *Merrill-Palmer Quarterly,* 1964, **10,** 249-263.

Dickens, C. *The adventures of Oliver Twist.* Boston: Aldine (In complete works of Dickens, undated).

Dingman, H. F. Adjustment of the mentally retarded on the community today. In G. A. Jervis (Ed.), *Expanding concepts in mental retardation: A symposium.* Springfield, Ill.: Charles C Thomas, 1968.

Dingman, H. F. A plea for social research in mental retardation. *American Journal of Mental Deficiency,* 1968, **73**(1), 2-4.

Dinnerstein, A. J. & Lowenthal, M. Teaching demonstrations of simulated disability. *Archives of Physical Medicine and Rehabilitation,* 1968, **49,** 167-170.

Dobbing, J. Early malnutrition in relation to development of brain and behavior. In B. W. Richards (Ed.), *Proceedings of the first international association for the scientific study of mental deficiency.* Surrey, England: Michael Jackson, Ltd., 1968.

Dobzhansky, T. Changing man. *Science,* 1967, **155**(3761), 509-415.

Dokecki, P. Review of the literature relative to the behavior potential of the severely retarded. *Training School Bulletin,* 1964, **61,** 65-75.

Doll, E. A. The essentials of an inclusive concept of mental deficiency. *American Journal of Mental Deficiency,* 1941, **46,** 214.

Doll, E. A. *The measurement of social competence: A manual for the Vineland social maturity scale.* Minneapolis: Educational Testing Bureau, 1953.

Doll, E. E. Trends and problems in the education of the mentally retarded: 1800-1940. *American Journal of Mental Deficiency,* 1967, **72**(2), 175-183.

Duche, D. J., & Lortholary, O. Les arrieres profounds psychotiques: Les traits psychotiques des arrieres profounds. In B. W. Richards (Ed.), *Proceedings of the first congress of the international association for the scientific study of mental deficiency.* Surrey, England: Michael Jackson, Ltd., 1968.

Doubros, S. G. Behavior therapy with high level, institutionalized, retarded adolescents. *Exceptional Children,* 1966, **33,** 229-233.

Doubros, S. G., & Daniels, G. J. An experimental approach to the reduction of overactive behavior. *Behavior Research & Therapy,* 1966, **4,** 251-258.

Douglas, J., & Bloomfield, J. *Children under fire.* London: Allen & Unwin, 1958.

Edgerton, R. B. *The cloak of competence.* Berkeley: University of California Press, 1967.

Edmonson, B., deJung, J. E., Leland, H., & Leach, E. M. *Test of social inference.* Freeport, New York: Educational Activities, 1974.

Edmonson, B., Leach, E. M., & Leland, H. *Social perceptual training for community living.* Freeport, New York: Activity Records, 1969.

Edmonson, B., Leland, H., deJung, J. E., & Leach, E. M. Increasing social cue interpretations (visual decoding) by retarded adolescents through training. *American Journal of Mental Deficiency,* 1967, **71,** 1017-1024.

Edmonson, B., Leland, H., & Leach, E. M. *Social inference training of retarded adolescents at the prevocational level.* Final Report of Research and Demonstration Project, 1968, University of Kansas Medical Center, Grant No. RD 1388, Vocational Rehabilitation Administration.

Edwards, M., & Lilly, R. T. Operant conditioning: An application to behavioral problems in groups. *Mental Retardation,* 1966, **4,** 18-20.

Eichenwald, H. F. *The prevention of mental retardation through control of infectious diseases.* June 9-11, 1966, Bethesda, Maryland, Public Health Service 1692, National Institute of Child Health and Human Development.

Eichenwald, H. F., & Fry, P. C. Nutrition and learning. *Science,* 1969, **163**(3868), 644-648.

Ellis, N. R. (Ed.). *International review of research in mental retardation.* New York: Academic Press, 1966-1971, 4 Vols.

Ellis, J. R., & Delhanty, J. E. A. Chromosomal translocation in mongolism and in normal relatives. *Lancet,* 1960, **11,** 409-410.

Elmer, E. *Children in jeopardy.* Pittsburgh: University of Pittsburgh Press, 1967.

Elonen, A. D., Polzien, M., & Zwarensteyn, S. B. The "uncommitted" blind child: Results of intensive training of children formally committed to institutions for the retarded. *Exceptional Children,* 1967, **33,** 301-307.

Ennis, B. J., & Friedman, P. R. (Eds.) *Legal rights of the mentally retarded.* Vol. 1. *Cases.* New York: Practicing Law Institute Mental Health Law Project, 1974.

Erdman, R. L., & Olson, J. L. Relationships between educational programs for the mentally retarded and the culturally deprived. *Mental Retardation Abstracts,* 1966, **3**(3), 311-318.

Ernhart, C. B., Graham, F. K., Eichman, P. L., Marshall, J. M., & Thurston, D. Brain injury in the preschool child: Some developmental considerations. Part II Comparison of brain injured and normal children. *Psychological Monographs,* 1963, **77**(11, Whole No. 574).

Eyman, R. K. Use and construction of data banks in mental retardation: Second report of the AAMD ad hoc committee. *American Journal of Mental Deficiency,* 1969, **74**(3), 441-447.

Eyman, R. K., Moore, B. C., Capes, L., & Zachofsky, T. Maladaptive behavior in institutionalized retardates with seizures. *American Journal of Mental Deficiency,* 1970, **74**(5), 651-659.

Fanon, F. *The wretched of the earth.* New York: Grove Press, 1968.

Farber, B. Perceptions of crisis and related variables in the impact of a retarded child on the mother. *Journal of Health and Human Behavior,* 1960, **1,** 108-118.

Farber, B. *Mental retardation: Its social context and social consequences.* Boston: Houghton Mifflin, 1968.

Fenton, J., & Thompson, M. M. The process of organizing a program for the employment of the mentally retarded, a state civil service system. *Rehabilitation Literature,* 1967, **28**(1), 2-8.

Fisher, L. Attention deficit in brain damaged children. *American Journal of Mental Deficiency,* 1970, **74**(4), 502-508.

Fitzsimmons, S. J., Cheever, J., Leonard, E., & Macunovich, D. School failures: Now and tomorrow. *Developmental Psychology,* 1969, **1**(2), 134-146.

Forsfman, H., & Lehmann, O. Chromosome studies in 11 families with mongolism in more than one member. *Acta Pediatrica,* 1962, **51,** 180-188.

Foster, R., & Nihira, K. Adaptive behavior as a measure of psychiatric impairment. *American Journal of Mental Deficiency,* 1969, **74**(3), 401-404.

Frostig, M. *Treatment of learning disorders in children.* 61st Ross Conference on Pediatric Research, Ross Laboratories, Columbus, Ohio (Library of Congress No. 53-22189), 1970, 118-122.

Frostig, M., & Horne, P. *The Frostig program for the Development of visual perception.* Chicago: Follet Publishing, 1964.

Frostig, M., & Horne, P. An approach to the treatment of children with learning disorders. In J. Hellmuth (Ed.), *Learning disorders.* Vol. 1. Seattle: Special Child Publications, 1965.

Gallagher, U. M. The adoption of mentally retarded children. *Children,* 1968, **15**(1), 17-21.

Gardner, J. M. Behavior modification research in mental retardation: Search for an adequate paradigm. *American Journal of Mental Deficiency,* 1969, **73**(6), 844-851.

Gardner, W. J. Use of punishment procedures with the severely retarded: A review. *American Journal of Mental Deficiency,* 1969, **74**(1), 86-103.

Gentry, J. T., Parkhurst, E., & Bulin, G. Z., Jr. An epidemiological study of congenital malformations in New York State. *American Journal on Public Health,* 1959, **49**(4), 497-513.

Giles, D. K., & Wolfe, M. M. Toilet training institutionalized, severe retardates: An application of operant behavior modification techniques. *American Journal of Mental Deficiency,* 1966, **70**(5), 766-780.

Girardeau, F. L. *The contribution of research to the improvement of programs for children and youth.* Paper presented at the Missouri-Kansas Psychological Association Meeting, Kansas City, Kansas, April 1968.

Girardeau, F. L. What is intelligence? *Mental Retardation,* 1969, **7**(1), 56-57.

Girardeau, F. L., & Spradlin, J. E. Token rewards in a cottage program. *Mental Retardation,* 1964, **21,** 345-351.

Gittelman, M., & Birch, H. G. Childhood schizophrenia: Intellect, neurologic status, perinatal risk, prognosis, family pathology. *Archives of General Psychiatry,* 1967, **17,** 16-25.

Goddard, H. H. *The Kallikak family: A study in the heredity of feeblemindedness.* New York: Macmillan, 1912.

Gold, E., Stone, M. L., & Rich, H. Total maternal and infant care: An evaluation. *American Journal on Public Health,* 1969, **59**(10), 1851-1856.

Goodman, M. *The role of the community agency in the integration of educable retardates in normal groups.* Paper presented at the meeting of Council for Exceptional Children, Denver, April 1969.

Gordon, S. Sense and nonsense about brain injury and learning disabilities. *Academic Therapy,* 1970, **1**(4), 249-254.

Gorki, M. The lower depths (translator Henry Burke) (1903). In R. W. Corrigan (Ed.), *The modern theatre.* New York: Macmillan, 1964.

Goslin, D. A. Standardized ability tests and testing. *Science,* 1968, **159** (3817), 851-856.

Graham, F. K., Ernhart, C. B., Craft, M., & Berman, B. W. Brain injury in the preschool child: Some developmental considerations: I Performance of normal children. *Psychological Monographs,* 1963, **77**(10, Whole No. 573).

Graham, F. K., & Kendall, B. S. *Memory for designs test.* Los Angeles: Psychological Tests Specialists, 1960.

Grossberg, J. M. Behavior therapy: A review. *Psychological Bulletin,* 1964, **62,** 77-88.

Grossman, H. (Ed.) *A manual on terminology and classification in mental retardation.* Special Publication Series No. 2. Washington, D. C.: American Association on Mental Deficiency, 1973.

Gunzburg, H. C. The assessment and evaluation of social development in the mentally handicapped child. In B. W. Richards (Ed.), *Proceedings of the first congress of the international association for the scientific study of mental deficiency.* Surrey, England: Michael Jackson, Ltd., 1968.

Haller, M. H. *Eugenics.* New Brunswick, N. J.: Rutgers University Press, 1963.

Halstead, W., & Rennick, P. Perception-cognition dissidences in children. In A. Kidd & R. Rivoire (Eds.), *Perceptual development in children.* New York: International Universities Press, 1966.

Hamilton, J., Stephens, L., & Allen, P. Controlling aggressive and destructive behavior in severely retarded, institutionalized residents. *American Journal of Mental Deficiency,* 1967, **71**(5), 852-856.

Haring, N. G. *Educating children who have epilepsy.* Washington, D. C.: The Epilepsy Foundation, 1959.

Haring, N. G., & Phillips, E. L. *Educating emotionally disturbed children.* New York: McGraw-Hill, 1962.

Haywood, H. C. Motivational orientation of over achieving and under achieving elementary school children. *American Journal of Mental Deficiency,* 1968, **72**(5), 662-667.

Haywood, H. C. Mental retardation as an extension of the developmental laboratory. *American Journal of Mental Deficiency,* 1970, **75**(1), 5-9.

Heber, R. (Ed.) A manual on terminology and classification in mental retardation. (2nd ed.) *American Journal of Mental Deficiency,* 1961, **66**(Monogr. Suppl.).

Heber, R. (Ed.) *Vocational rehabilitation of the mentally retarded.* Vocational Rehabilitation Administration, Rehabilitation Series, No. 65-16, Washington, D. C.: U. S. Government Printing Office, 1963.

Heber, R. The role of environmental variables in the etiology of culture-familial mental retardation. In B. W. Richards (Ed.), *Proceedings of the first congress of the international association for the scientific study of mental deficiency.* Surrey, England: Michael Jackson, Ltd., 1968.

Heinstein, M. I. Behavioral correlates of breast-bottle regimes under varying parent-infant relationships. *Monographs of the Society for Research and Child Development,* 1963, No. 4.

Helfer, R. E., & Kempe, C. H. *The battered child.* Chicago: University of Chicago Press, 1968.

Hendriksen, K., & Doughty, R. Decelerating undesired meal time behavior in a group of profoundly retarded boys. *American Journal of Mental Deficiency,* 1967, **72**(1), 40-44.

Hermelin, B. Immediate verbal recall in autistic children. In B. W. Richards (Ed.), *Proceedings of the first congress of the international association for the scientific study of mental deficiency.* Surrey, England: Michael Jackson, Ltd., 1968.

Hinton, G., & Knights, R. M. *Neurological and psychological characteristics of 100 children with seizures.* Research Bulletin No. 57, Department of Psychology, University of Western Ontario, London, Canada, 1966.

Hollis, J. H. The effects of social and nonsocial stimuli on the behavior of profoundly retarded children: Part I. *American Journal of Mental Deficiency,* 1965, **69,** 755-771. (a)

Hollis, J. H. The effects of social nonsocial stimuli on the behavior of profoundly retarded children: Part II. *American Journal of Mental Deficiency,* 1965, **69,** 772-789. (b)

Hormone and Behavior, 1969, **1**(1). New York: Academic Press.

Ingalls, T. H., Curley, F. J., & Prindle, R. A. Experimental production of congenital anomalies: Timing and degree of anoxia as factors causing fetal deaths and congenital anomalies. *New England Journal of Medicine,* 1952, **247,** 758-768.

Jabbour, J. T. Indications for psychological evaluation in mental retardation and neurological disorders. In J. L. Khanna (Ed.), *Brain damage and mental retardation.* Springfield, Ill.: Charles C Thomas, 1968.

Jacobs, A., & Weingold, J. G. *The sheltered workshop: A community rehabilitation source on mentally retarded.* New York: Bureau of Publications, Teachers College, Columbia University, 1958.

Jacobs, P., Baikie, A. D., Court-Brown, W. M., & Strong, J. A. The somatic chromosomes in mongolism. *Lancet,* 1959, **11,** 7-10.

Jacobs, P. A., & Strong, J. A. A case of human intersexuality having a possible XXY sex-determining mechanism. *Nature,* 1959, **183,** 302-303.

Jedrysek, E., Rosenblatt, J. S., & Wortis, J. Social class influences on intellectual development. In B. W. Richards (Ed.), *Proceedings of the first congress of international association of scientific study of mental deficiency.* Surrey, England: Michael Jackson, Ltd., 1968.

Jensen, A. R. How much can we boost IQ and scholastic achievement? *Educational Review,* 1969, **39**(1), 1-123.

Johnson, B., & Morse, H. A. Injured children and their parents. *Children,* 1968, **15**(4), 147-152.

Johnson, G. O. Psychological characteristics of the mentally retarded. In W. M. Cruickshank (Ed.), *Psychology of exceptional children and youth.* Englewood Cliffs, N. J.: Prentice-Hall, 1963.

Journal of Applied Behavior Analysis, 1970, **1.**

Kalter, H., & Warkany, J. Experimental production of congenital malformations in mammals by metabolic procedure. *Physiological Reviews,* 1959, **39**(1), 69-115.

Kanner, L. Parents' feelings about retarded children. *American Journal of Mental Deficiency,* 1953, **57,** 375-383. (a)

Kanner, L. Mental Health in child rearing. *Child,* 1953, **17,** 116-117. (b)

Kanner, L. *A history of care and study of the mentally retarded.* Springfield, Ill.: Charles C Thomas, 1964.

Kanner, L. Medicine in the history of mental retardation: 1800-1965. *American Journal of Mental Deficiency,* 1967, **72**(2), 165-170.

Kaplan, A. R. The use of cytogenetical data in heredity counseling. *American Journal of Mental Deficiency,* 1969, **73**(4), 636-653.

Katz, E. *The retarded adult in the community.* Springfield, Ill.: Charles C Thomas, 1968.

Katz, E. (Ed.). *Mental health services for the mentally retarded.* Springfield, Ill.: Charles C Thomas, 1972.

Kennedy, J. F. *Mental illness and mental retardation.* Message from the President of the United States relative to mental illness and mental retardation. Feb. 5, 1963, presented to the 88th Congress, House of Representatives, U. S. Document No. 58.

Kershner, J. R. Intellectual and social development in relation to the family functioning: A longitudinal comparison of home vs. institutional effects. *American Journal of Mental Deficiency,* 1970, **75**(3), 276-284.

Kessler, J. Cognition. In J. Hellmuth (Ed.), *Cognitive studies.* New York: Brunner/Mazel, 1970.

Kidd, J. W. President's Page. *Exceptional Children,* 1968, **35,** 189.

Kinsbourne, M. *Neuropsychologic and neurophysiologic aspects of learning disorders and learning disorders in children.* 61st Ross Conference on Pediatric Research, Ross Laboratories, Columbus, Ohio (Library of Congress No. 53-22189), 1970.

Kirk, S. A. *The diagnosis and remediation of psycholinguistic abilities.* Urbana, Ill.: Institute for Research on Exceptional Children, 1966.

Klebanoff, L. B. Facilities for the mentally retarded: Integrated or separate but equal. *American Journal of Public Health,* 1964, **54**(2), 244-248.

Klinefelter, H. S., Jr., Reisenstein, E. C., & Albright, F. Syndrome characterized by gynaecomastia, aspermatogenesis without a- leydigism and increased excretion of follicle stimulating hormone. *Journal of Clinical Endocrinology,* 1942, **2,** 615.

Klosovsky, B. N. Development of the brain in cases of disorder of the endocrine glands and viscera during pregnancy. In B. W. Richards (Ed.), *Proceedings of the first congress of the international association for the scientific study of mental deficiency.* Surrey, England: Michael Jackson, Ltd., 1968.

Knights, R. M., & Hinton, G. G. *Minimal brain dysfunction: Clinical and psychological test characteristics.* Research Bulletin No. 56, Dept. of Psychology, University of Western Ontario, London, Canada, 1967.

Knights, R. M., & Ogilvie, R. M. *A comparison of test results from normal and brain damaged children.* Research Bulletin No. 53, Dept. of Psychology, University of Western Ontario, London, Canada, 1967.

Knights, R. M., & Watson, P. *The use of computer test profiles in neuropsychological assessment.* Research Bulletin No. 71, Dept. of Psychology, University of Western Ontario, London, Canada, 1968.

Knobloch, H., Pasamanick, B., Harper, P. A., & Rider, R. V. The effect of prematurity on health and growth. *American Journal on Public Health,* 1959, **49**(9), 1164-1173.

Krasner, L., & Ullman, L. P. (Eds.) *Research in behavior modification: New developments and implications.* New York: Holt, Rinehart & Winston, 1965.

Kugel, R. B., & Parsons, M. H. *Children of deprivation.* Children's Bureau Publication No. 440. Washington, D. C.: Dept. of Health, Education, and Welfare, 1967.

Kugel, R. B., & Wolfensberger, W. (Eds.) *Changing patterns in residential services for the mentally retarded.* Washington, D. C.: President's Committee on Mental Retardation, 1969.

Kurtz, R. A., & Wolfensberger, W. Cultural deprivation, lower class and mental retardation: Certain terminological and conceptual confusion. *Social Science and Medicine,* 1969, **3,** 229-237.

Lamp, R., & Yater, A. C. Heterogeneity of intellectual performance by disadvantaged children within a metropolitan area. Mimeograph, St. Louis University, 1968.

Leland, Helen. The language of mental differences. *Project News,* 1968, **4**(1), 1-5. Parsons State Hospital and Training Center, Parsons, Kansas.

Leland, Henry. Some psychological characteristics of phenylketonuria. *Psychological Reports,* 1957, **3,** 373-376.

Leland, H. What is a mentally retarded child? *Journal of Psychiatric Nursing,* 1964, **2**(1), 21-36.

Leland, H. *Mental retardation tomorrow, in issues: Challenges for change.* In E. G. Sutter (Ed.), *Presidential Address* Proceedings of the Oct. 1968 Meeting of American Association of Mental Deficiency, Region V, AAMD, Houston, Texas, October 1968.

Leland, H. The relationship between 'intelligence' and mental retardation. *American Journal of Mental Deficiency,* 1969, **73,** 533-535. (a)

Leland, H. Standards for bricks or people. *Clinical Child Psychology Newsletter,* 1969, **8**(1), 5-7. (b)

Leland, H. Adaptive behavior and mentally retarded behavior. In G. Tarjan, R. K. Eyman, & C. E. Meyers (Eds.), *Sociobehavioral research service in mental retardation—papers in honor of Harvey F. Dingman.* AAMD Monograph Series No. 1, 1973. (a)

Leland, H. The neighborhood center concept for the retarded. *Journal of Clinical Child Psychology,* 1973, **11**(1), 25-27. (b)

Leland, H., & Goldberg, I. Rehabilitation of the institutionalized mentally retarded. *American Psychologist,* 1957, **12,** 528-530.

Leland, H., Nihira, K., Foster, R., & Shellhaas, M. The demonstration and measurement of adaptive behavior. In B. W. Richards (Ed.), *Proceedings of the first congress of the international association for the scientific study of mental deficiency.* Surrey, England: Michael Jackson, Ltd., 1968.

Leland, H., Nihira, K., Foster, R., Shellhaas, M., & Kagin, E. *Conference on measurement of adaptive behavior:* III. NIMH Grant No. MH 14901, Parsons State Hospital and Training Center, Parsons, Kansas, April 1968.

Leland, H., & Smith, D. E. *Play therapy with mentally subnormal children.* New York: Grune and Stratton, 1965.

Leland, H., & Smith, D. E. Psychotherapeutic considerations with mentally retarded and developmentally disabled children. In E. Katz (Ed.), *Mental health services for the mentally retarded.* Springfield, Ill.: Charles C Thomas, 1972.

Leland, H., Smith, D. E., & Barclay, A. Report of the workshop on the training of clinical child psychologists in mental retardation. *Mental Retardation,* 1970, **4**(8), 24-28.

Leland, H., Shellhaas, M., Nihira, K., & Foster, R. Adaptive behavior: A new dimension in the classification of the mentally retarded. *Mental Retardation Abstracts,* 1967, **4**(3), 359-387.

Lemkau, P. V., & Imre, P. D. Results of a field epidemologic study. *American Journal of Mental Deficiency,* 1969, **73**(6), 858-863.

Lenneberg, E. H. *Biological foundations of language.* New York: John Wiley & Sons, 1967.

Lennox, W. G. *Epilepsy and related disorders.* 2 Vols. Boston: Little, Brown, 1960.

Lent, J., LeBlanc, J., & Spradlin, J. A demonstration program for intensive training of institutionalized mentally retarded girls. *Project News,* 1967, **3**(2), 1-18. Parsons State Hospital and Training Center, Parsons, Kansas.

Levi, A. Treatment of a disorder of perception and concept formation in a case of school failure. *Journal of Consulting Psychology,* 1965, **29**-(4), 289-295.

Lewis, O. The culture of poverty. *Scientific American,* 1966, **215**(4), 19-25.

Liberthson, E. Helping families live with and for the mentally retarded child. *Journal of Rehabilitation,* 1968, **34**(6), 24-26.

Lincoln-Oseretsky Motor Development Scale. Los Angeles: Western Psychological Services, 1955.

Lindsley, O. R. An experiment with parents handling behavior at home. *Johnstone Bulletin,* 1966, **9,** 27-36. Johnstown Training Center, Bordentown, New Jersey.

lin-Fu, J. S. *Rubella.* Washington, D. C.: Dept. of Health, Education, and Welfare, Children's Bureau, 1968.

Lloyd, L. L., & Frisina, R. D. *The audiologic assessment of the mentally retarded: Proceedings of a national conference.* Parsons State Hospital and Training Center, Parsons, Kansas, March 1965.

Lloyd, L. L., & Reid, M. J. The incidence of hearing impairment in an institutionalized mentally retarded population. *American Journal of Mental Deficiency,* 1967, **71**(5), 746-763.

Lowenfeld, B. Psychological problems of children with impaired vision. In W. M. Cruickshank (Ed.), *Psychology of exceptional children and youth.* (2nd ed.) Englewood Cliffs, N. J.: Prentice-Hall, 1963.

Lucero, R. J., Vail, D. J., & Scherber, J. Regulating operant conditioning programs. *Hospital and Community Psychiatry,* 1968, **19,** 41-42.

Luszki, W. A. Hearing loss and intelligence among retardates. *American Journal of Mental Deficiency,* 1965, **70**(1), 92-101.

Luther, M. *Colloquia Mensalia.* London: William Du-gard, 1652.

MacAndrew, C., & Edgerton, R. On the possibility of friendship. *American Journal of Mental Deficiency,* 1966, **70**(4), 612-621.

Machover, K. *Personality projection in drawings of the human figure.* Springfield, Ill.: Charles C Thomas, 1949.

Mackey, R. W. Problems in evaluation of residual effects of head injury. In J. L. Khanna (Ed.), *Brain damage and mental retardation.* Springfield, Ill.: Charles C Thomas, 1968.

Mackinnon, D. W. The structure of personality. In J. McV. Hunt (Ed.), *Personality and the behavior disorders.* Vol. 1. New York: Ronald Press, 1944.

MacLeech, B. A forward looking concept in rehabilitation; reflections on the young adult institute. *7th Annual Distinguished Lecture Series,* University of Southern California, Los Angeles, 1968.

Magoun, H. W., Darling, L., & Prost, J. The evolution of man's brain. In M. Brazier (Ed.), *The central nervous system and behavior.* New York: Josiah Macy, Jr., Foundation, 1960.

Mandelbaum, A., & Wheeler, M. E. The meaning of a defective child to parents. *Social Casework,* 1960, **41,** 360-367.

Martin, H. Child abuse in Kansas. *Community Health,* 1968, **2**(5), 4-6.

Mauer, E. Chromosome and Genome as conceptual models for certain types of mental retardation. *American Journal of Mental Deficiency,* 1965, **70**(2), 191-203.

McCarthy, J. J., & Scheerenberger, R. C. A decade of research on the education of the mentally retarded. *Mental Retardation Abstracts,* 1966, **3**(4), 481-501.

McCarthy, J. J., & McCarthy, J. F. *Learning Disabilities.* Boston: Allyn & Bacon, 1969.

McDonald, E. T. *Understand those feelings.* Pittsburgh: Stanwix House, 1962.

McGaugh, J. L. Time-dependent processes in memory storage. *Science,* 1966, **153,** 1351-1358.

McWhirter, K. XYY chromosomes and criminal acts. Letter in *Science,* 1969, **164,** 1117.

Mercer, J. R. Patterns of family crisis related to reacceptance of the retardate. *American Journal of Mental Deficiency,* 1966, **71**(1), 19-32.

Milgram, N. A. A rationale and irrational in Zigler's motivational approach to mental retardation. *American Journal of Mental Deficiency,* 1969, **73**(4), 527-533.

Miller, S. A. Short comments. In N. Scrimshaw & J. Gordon (Eds.), *Malnutrition, learning, and behavior.* Cambridge, Mass.: Massachusetts Institute of Technology, 1968.

Mitchell, A. C., & Smeriglio, V. Growth in social competence in institutionalized mentally retarded children. *American Journal of Mental Deficiency,* 1970, **74**(5), 666-673.

Moore, B. C. Relationship between prematurity and intelligence in mental retardates. *American Journal of Mental Deficiency,* 1965, **70**(3), 448-453.

Morris, N. M., Hatch, M. H., & Chapman, S. S. Deterrents to well child supervision. *American Journal on Public Health,* 1966, **56**(8), 1232-1241.

Mosier, H. D., Jr., Grossman, H. J., & Dingman, H. F. Physical growth in mental defectives. *Pediatrics,* 1965, **36**(3, Part 2), 465-519.

Murphy, W. K., & Scheerenberger, R. C. Day care centers for the mentally retarded. In J. Rothstein (Ed.), *Mental retardation readings and resources.* (2nd ed.) New York: Holt, Rinehart & Winston, 1971.

Mykelbust, H. R. The deaf child with other handicaps. *American Annals of the Deaf,* 1958, **103,** 496-509.

Nachman, R. *Drug influences in mental retardation.* Paper presented at the meeting of the American Association on Mental Deficiency, Houston, June 1971.

National Institute of Mental Health. *Essential services of the community mental health center.* Washington, D. C.: Dept. of Health, Education, and Welfare. Public Health Service Publication Nos. 1449, 1477, 1478, 1578, & 1624.

Neurological and sensory disease control program. Minimal dysfunction national project on learning disabilities in children. Washington, D. C.: Dept. of Health, Education, and Welfare. Public Health Service Publication No. 2015, 1969.

New York State Department of Mental Hygiene. A special census of suspected referred mental retardation, Onondaga County, New York. In *Technical Report of the Mental Health Research Unit,* New York State Department of Mental Hygiene, Albany, 1955, 84-127.

Nichols, P. *Joe Egg.* New York: Grove Press, 1967.

Nihira, K. Factorial dimensions of adaptive behavior in adult retardates. *American Journal of Mental Deficiency,* 1969, **73**(6), 868-878. (a)

Nihira, K. Factorial dimensions of adaptive behavior in mentally retarded children and adolescents. *American Journal of Mental Deficiency,* 1969, **74**(1), 130-141. (b)

Nihira, K., Foster, R., & Spencer, L. Measurement of adaptive behavior: A descriptive system for mental retardates. *American Journal of Orthopsychiatry,* 1968, **38**(4), 622-634.

Nirje, B. The Normalization principle and its human management implications. In R. B. Kugel & W. Wolfensberger (Eds.), *Changing patterns in residential services for the mentally retarded.* Washington, D. C.: President's Committee on Mental Retardation, 1969.

O'Connor, G., Justice, R. S., & Warren, N. The aged mentally retarded: Institution or community care. *American Journal of Mental Deficiency,* 1970, **75**(3), 354-360.

Olivier, K., & Barclay, A. Stanford-Binet and Goodenough Harris Test performance of Head Start children. *Psychological Reports,* 1967, **20,** 1175-1179.

Olshansky, S. Parent responses to a mentally defective child. *Mental Retardation,* 1966, **4**(4), 21-23.

Ostrom, T. M., Rosenblood, L. K., & Hubbard, J. Important hierarchy of AAMD standards for residential institutions. *Mental Retardation,* 1971, **2**(1), 29-32.

Overly, M. W. Lead poisoning: A preventable childhood disease of the slums. *Science,* 1969, **165**(3897), 991-992.

Payne, G. H. *The child in human progress.* New York: G. P. Putman & Sons, 1916.

Penfield, W. Memory mechanisms. *Archives of Neurology and Psychiatry,* 1952, **67,** 178-198.

Pevzner, M. S. *Oliogophrenia: Mental Deficiency in children.* J. Wortis (Ed.), International Behavioral Sciences Series. New York: Consutant's Bureau, 1959.

Piotrowski, Z. A. A Rorschach compendium revised and enlarged. *Psychiatric Quarterly,* 1950, **24,** 543-596.

Pond, D. A. Epilepsy and mental deficiency. In B. W. Richards, A. D. B. Clarke, & A. Shapiro (Eds.), *Proceedings of the London conference on the scientific study of mental deficiency.* Vol. 1. Dangenham, England: May and Baker Ltd., 1962.

Pond, D. A. Psychiatric aspects of epileptic and brain damaged children. *British Medical Journal,* 1961, **2,** 1377-1382, 1454-1459.

Poole, B. D. Mental retardation and maternal and child health programs. *American Journal on Public Health,* 1965, **55**(1), 27-32.

Premack, D. Reinforcement theory. In D. Levine (Ed.), *Nebraska symposium on motivation.* Lincoln: University of Nebraska Press, 1965.

President's committee on mental retardation and bureau of education for the handicapped. *The six hour retarded child.* Washington, D. C.: U. S. Government Printing Office, Dept. of Health, Education, and Welfare, Office of Education, 1970.

President's panel on mental retardation. *A proposed program for national action to combat mental retardation.* Washington, D. C.: U. S. Government Printing Office, 1962.

Pribram, K. H., & Tubbs, W. E. Short-term memory parsing and the primate frontal cortex. *Science,* 1966, **156**(3783), 1765-1767.

Pribram, K. H. The neurophysiology of remembering. *Scientific American,* 1969, (1), 73-86.

Price, W. H., & Whatmore, P. B. Behavior disorders and pattern of crime among XYY males identified at a maximum security hospital. *British Medical Journal,* 1967, **1,** 533. (a)

Price, W. H., & Whatmore, P. B. Criminal behavior and the XYY male. *Nature,* London, 1967, **213,** 815. (b)

Provence, S., & Lipton, R. C. *Infants in institutions.* New York: International Universities Press, 1962.

Pumphrey, M. W., & Peters, E. N. *The behavior characteristics of educable retarded school children in social interaction with their normal peers.* Paper presented at the meeting of Council of Exceptional Children, Denver, Colorado (Supported by MH 14424, Integration of Educable Retardates in Normal Groups), Jewish Community Centers Association of St. Louis, St. Louis, Mo., April 1969.

Rapaport, D. *Emotions and memory.* New York: International Universities Press, 1959 (Menninger Clinic Monograph Series No. 2).

Reed, H. B. C., Jr., & Fitzhugh, K. B. Patterns of deficits in relationship to severity of cerebral dysfunction in children and adults. *Journal of Consulting Psychology,* 1966, **30**(2), 98-102.

Reitan, R. M. A research program on the psychological effects of brain lesions in human beings. In N. R. Ellis (Ed.), *International review of research in mental retardation.* New York: Academic Press, 1966.

Rennick, P. M. The neurologically impaired child: The problem of evaluation. *Proceedings, Symposium on Neurologically Impaired Children.* Tempe: Arizona State University Press, 1966.

Risley, T. Learning and lollipops. *Psychology Today,* 1968, (1), 1-28.

Robinson, H. B., & Robinson, N. M. *The mentally retarded child.* New York: McGraw-Hill, 1965.

Rosenthal, R., & Jacobson, L. F. Teacher expectations for the disadvantaged. *Scientific American,* 1968, **218**(4), 19-24.

Ross, S. A. Effects of intentional training in social behavior on retarded children. *American Journal of Mental Deficiency,* 1969, **73**(6), 912-920.

Roth, W. B. *Listing of operating federal assistance programs compiled during the Roth study.* 90th Congress, House of Representatives, Document No. 399. Washington, D. C.: U. S. Government Printing Office, 1968.

Rothstein, J. H. *Mental retardation.* (2nd ed.) New York: Holt, Rinehart & Winston, 1971.

Royal commission on the law relating to mental illness and mental deficiency, 1954-1957. Report. London: Her Majesty's Stationary Office, 1957.

Rubella: The study puts defect rate at almost 90%. *World Medical News,* 1967 (September 19).

Rudin, E. Comprehensive centers for the mentally retarded. *American Journal on Public Health,* 1964, **54**(12), 1977-1981.

Sanders, B., Zigler, E., & Butterfield, H. C. Outer-Directedness in the discrimination learning of normal and mentally retarded children. *Journal of Abnormal Psychology,* 1968, **73,** 368-375.

Scheerenberger, R. C. Nursery school experiences for the mentally retarded. In J. H. Rothstein (Ed.), *Mental retardation readings and resources.* (2nd ed.) New York: Holt, Rinehart & Winston, 1971.

Schiefelbusch, R. L., Bair, H. V., & Spradlin, J. E. Language studies of mentally retarded children. *Journal of Speech and Hearing Disorders,* 1963, (Monogr. Suppl. 10).

Schweitzer, M. *Current bibliography of epidemiology.* Vol. 1 (5). New York: American Public Health Association, 1969.

Scrimshaw, N., & Gordon, J. (Eds.) *Malnutrition, learning, and behavior.* Proceedings of and International Conference, March 1-3, 1967, cosponsored by the Nutrition Foundation, Inc., and The Massachusetts Institute of Technology, Cambridge, Massachusetts, 1968.

Secretary's Committee on Mental Retardation. *Mental retardation activities.* Washington, D. C.: Department of Health, Education, and Welfare, January 1968.

SEICUS. *A resource guide in sex education for the mentally retarded.* New York: Sex Education and Information Council of the United States, 1971.

Shellhaas, M. D. The effects of small groups interaction of sociometric choices of day campers. *American Journal of Mental Deficiency,* 1969, **74**(2), 259-263. (a)

Shellhaas, M. D. Sociometric status of institutionalized retarded children and nonretarded community children. *American Journal of Mental Deficiency,* 1969, **73**(5), 804-808. (b)

Shellhaas, M. D., & Nihira, K. Factor analysis comparison of reasons retardates are institutionalized in two populations. *American Journal of Mental Deficiency,* 1970, **74**(5), 626-632.

Shellhaas, M. D., & Nihira, K. Factor analysis of reasons retardates are referred to an institution. *American Journal of Mental Deficiency,* 1969, **74**(2), 171-179.

Sheltered workshops for the mentally retarded. *Mental Retardation Abstracts,* 1965, **2**(4), 482-486.

Shuy, R. W. A linguistic background for developing beginning reading materials for black children. In J. C. Baratz, & R. W. Shuy (Eds.), *Teaching black children to read.* Washington, D. C.: Center for Applied Linguistics, 1969.

Simon, G. B. Anomalies of growth in a group of children exhibiting psychotic features. *Journal of Mental Subnormality,* 1966, **12**(1), 42-44.

Skodak, M. Adult status in individuals who experienced early intervention. In B. W. Richards (Ed.), *Proceedings of the first congress of the international association for the study of mental deficiency.* Surrey, England: Michael Jackson, Ltd., 1968.

Smith, D. E. An experimental program for moderately and severely mentally retarded children. Unpublished master's thesis, Kansas State Teachers College, Pittsburg, Kansas, 1959.

Smith, M. B., & Hobbs, N. The community and the community health center. *American Psychologist,* 1966, **21**(60), 499-509.

Smith, R. M. Creative thinking abilities of educable mentally handicapped in regular grades. *American Journal of Mental Deficiency,* 1967, **71**(4), 571-575.

Smith, R. M. *An introduction to mental retardation.* New York: McGraw-Hill, 1971.

Snyder, R. D., & Worden, D. K. Failure of parental tutoring in childhood dyslexia. *Clinical Pediatrics,* 1969, **8**(8), 436.

Spearhead at Juniper Gardens. (Documentary Film) Bureau of Child Research, University of Kansas Bureau of Visual Instruction, Lawrence, Kansas, 1968.

Speijer, N. Basic principles of the sheltered workshop. In B. W. Richards (Ed.), *Proceedings of the first congress of the international association for the scientific study of mental deficiency.* Surrey, England: Michael Jackson, Ltd., 1968.

Stahlecker, L. V. Counseling parents of slow-learning children. *Community Mental Health Journal,* 1965, **1**(2), 171-174.

Sternlicht, M. Psychotherapeutic techniques useful with the mentally retarded: A review of critique. *The Psychiatric Quarterly,* 1965, **39,** 84-90.

Stoller, A. Virus action during meiosis or early mitosis in mothers as a possible cause of cogenital anomalies. In B. W. Richards (Ed.), *Proceedings of the first congress of the international association for the scientific study of mental deficiency.* Surrey, England: Michael Jackson, Ltd., 1968.

Strauss, A. A., & Kephart, N. *Psychopathology and education of the brain injured child:* Vol. 2, Progress in theory and clinic. New York: Grune & Stratton, 1955.

Strauss, A. A., & Lehtinen, L. E. *Psychopathology and education of the brain injured child.* Vol. 1. New York: Grune & Stratton, 1947.

Sutter, E., Leland, H., & Barclay, A. (Eds.) *Report of the workshop on the role of subprofessionals in clinical and child psychology in mental retardation.* Washington, D. C.: American Psychological Association, 1969.

Talkington, L. W., & Chiovaro, S. A. An approach to programming for aged. *Mental Retardation,* 1969, **7**(1), 29-30.

Thomas, A., Chess, S., & Birch, H. G. *Temperament and behavior disorders in children.* New York: New York University Press, 1968.

Thomas, A., Chess, S., Birch, H. G., Hertzig, M. E., & Korn, S. *Behavioral individuality in early childhood.* New York: New York University Press, 1963.

Tighe, T. J., & Elliott, R. A technique for controlling behavior in natural life settings. *Journal of Applied Behavior Analysis,* 1968, **1**(3), 263-266.

Tizard, B. The personality of epileptics: A discussion of the evidence. *Psychological Bulletin,* 1962, **59,** 196-210.

Toombs, L. E. Education and behavioral modification through the use of closed circuit television. *Project News,* 1967, **3**(3), 1-5. Parsons State Hospital and Training Center, Parsons, Kansas.

Townsend, T. *The last refuge—A survey of residential institutions and homes for the aged in England and Wales.* London: Routledge and Kegan, 1962.

Tsikoto, G. V. Role of games in developing visually formed thoughts in preschool aged MR children. *Spetsial-Naya Shkola,* 1968, **3**(129), 60-64.

Ullman, L., & Krasner, L. (Eds.) *Case studies in behavior modification.* New York: Holt, Rinehart & Winston, 1965.

Vail, D. J. *Dehumanization and the institutional career.* Springfield, Ill.: Charles C Thomas, 1967.

Veblen, T. *The theory of the leisure class.* New York: Modern Library, 1934.

Vernon, M., & Brown, D. W. A guide to psychological tests and testing procedures in the evaluation of deaf and hard of hearing children. *Journal of Speech and Hearing Disorders,* 1964, **29**(4), 414-423.

Von Haden, H. I., & King, J. M. *Educational Innovator's Guide.* Worthington, Ohio: Charles A. Jones, 1974.

Warner, A., Queen, S. A., & Harper, E. B. *American charities and social work.* (4th ed.) New York: Thomas C. Cowell, 1942.

Warren, S. A. *Behavioral modification in child therapy.* Symposium presented at the meeting of the American Psychological Association, Chicago, September 1965.

Warren, S. A. Psychological evaluation of the mentally retarded. In H. Grossman (Ed.), *Pediatric Clinics of North America,* 1968, **15**(4).

Watson, L. F., Jr. Programmed instruction with the retarded. *Mental Retardation Abstracts,* 1964, **1**(1), 28-29.

Weber, E. *Early childhood education: Perspectives on change.* Worthington, Ohio: Charles A. Jones, 1970.

Wechsler, D. *Wechsler intelligence scale for children: Manual.* New York: Psychological Corporation, 1949.

Weltfish, G. Some main trends in American anthropology in 1961. *Annals of American Academic Political and Social Science,* 1962, **33,** 171-176.

White, W. D. Planning and programming for the retarded yesterday, today, and tomorrow. In E. G. Sutter (Ed.), *Issues, challenges for change.* Proceedings of the 1968 meeting of American Association of Mental Deficiency, Region V, Richmond State School, Richmond, Texas, 1969.

Whitney, L. R., & Bernard, K. W. Implications of operant learning theory for nursing care of the retarded child. *Mental Retardation,* 1966, **4,** 26-29.

Williams, E. H. Effects of readiness on incidential learning in EMR, normal and gifted children. *American Journal of Mental Deficiency,* 1970, **72**(2), 117-119.

Winick, M. Malnutrition and cellular growth in the brain. Paper presented at the 78th Annual Meeting of American Psychological Association, Miami Beach, Florida, September 1970.

Witkin, H. A. Individual differences in ease of perception of embedded figures. *Journal of Personality,* 1950, **19,** 1-15.

Wolfe, M. M., Giles, D. K., & Hall, R. V. Experiments with token reinforcement in the remedial classroom. *Behavior Research and Therapy,* 1968, **6,** 51-64.

Wolfensberger, W. Counseling the parents of the retarded. In A. Baumeister (Ed.), *Mental retardation: Appraisal, education and rehabilitation.* Chicago: Aldine, 1967.

Wolfensberger, W. The origin and nature of our institutional models. In R. B. Kugel, & W. Wolfensberger (Eds.), *Changing patterns in residential services for the mentally retarded.* Washington, D. C.: President's Committee on Mental Retardation, 1969.

Woloshin, A. A., Tardi, G., & Tobin, A. De-Institutionalization of mentally retarded men through use of half-way house. *Mental Retardation,* 1966, **4**(3), 21-26.

Wolpe, J., & Lazarus, A. A. *Behavior therapy techniques: A guide to the treatment of neurosis.* Oxford, England: Pergamon Press, 1966.

Wortis, H., & Freedman, A. The contribution of social environment to the development of premature children. *American Journal of Orthopsychiatry,* 1965, **35**(1), 57-68.

Wortis, H. Poverty and retardation: Social aspects. In J. Wortis (Ed.), *Mental retardation: An annual review.* Vol. 1. New York: Grune & Stratton, 1970.

Wright, B. A. *Physical disability—A psychological approach.* New York: Harper & Row, 1960.

Yarrow, L. J. Conceptualizing the early environment. In L. L. Dittman (Ed.), *Early child care.* New York: Atherton Press, 1968.

Young, B. W. Head Start and other preschool enrichment programs. In J. S. Roucek (Ed.), *The slow learner.* New York: Philosophical Library, 1969.

Zaporozhets, A. V. *The development of voluntary movements.* Moscow: Academy of Pedagological Science, 1960. Cited by D. E. Berlyne, Soviet research on intellectual processes in children. In J. C. Wright, & J. Kagan (Eds.), *Basic cognitive processes in children.* Monographs of the Society for Research in Child Development, 1963, **28**(2).

Zigler, E. Familial mental retardation: A continuing dilemma. *Science,* 1967, **155**(3760), 292-298.

Zigler, E. Developmental versus difference theories of mental retardation and the problem of motivation. *American Journal of Mental Deficiency,* 1969, **73**(4), 535-556.

Zwerling, I. Initial counseling of parents with mentally retarded children. *Journal of Pediatrics,* 1954, **44**(4), 469-479.

Author Index

Subject Index